Malware Analysis in Cybersecurity

James Relington

DEDICATION

To those who tirelessly safeguard digital systems, ensuring security and trust in an ever-evolving digital world—this book is dedicated to you. Your commitment to protecting access, enforcing governance, and navigating the complexities cybersecurity is invaluable. May this work serve as a guide and inspiration in your ongoing efforts to create a more secure and compliant future.

AKNOWLEDGEMENTS

I extend my deepest gratitude to everyone who contributed to the creation of this book. To my colleagues and mentors in the field of identity governance, your insights and expertise have been invaluable. To my friends and family, your unwavering support and encouragement have made this journey possible. To the professionals and innovators dedicated to securing digital identities, your work continues to inspire and shape the future of cybersecurity. This book is a reflection of collective knowledge, and I am grateful to all who have played a role in its development.

Introduction to Malware Analysis

Malware analysis is a critical field in cybersecurity that focuses on understanding, dissecting, and mitigating malicious software. With the rise of sophisticated cyber threats, analyzing malware has become an essential skill for security professionals, incident responders, and researchers. The goal of malware analysis is to determine how a piece of malware operates, what damage it can cause, and how to defend against it. This process involves different techniques, ranging from basic static analysis to advanced reverse engineering, each providing valuable insights into the behavior and intent of the malware.

Malware, short for malicious software, is designed to disrupt, damage, or gain unauthorized access to computer systems. It can take many forms, including viruses, worms, Trojans, ransomware, spyware, and rootkits. Cybercriminals use malware for various purposes, such as stealing sensitive information, controlling infected systems remotely, or launching large-scale cyberattacks. As technology evolves, so do the techniques used by attackers, making it crucial for analysts to stay ahead by continuously refining their skills and methodologies.

The process of malware analysis begins with obtaining a sample, often from an infected system, network traffic, or threat intelligence reports. Analysts must ensure that the sample is handled in a secure environment, typically within a controlled lab setup that prevents accidental infections. A malware analysis lab usually consists of isolated virtual machines, network monitoring tools, and specialized software for examining malicious code. This controlled setup allows analysts to safely execute and observe malware behavior without risking unintended spread or damage.

There are two primary approaches to malware analysis: static analysis and dynamic analysis. Static analysis involves examining the malware sample without executing it. Analysts inspect the file's structure, metadata, and embedded strings to gather preliminary information. Tools such as PEStudio and Binwalk help extract useful details, such as API calls, embedded URLs, or encryption keys. While static analysis is a quick and relatively safe method, it has limitations, especially when dealing with obfuscated or packed malware designed to evade detection.

Dynamic analysis, on the other hand, involves executing the malware in a controlled environment to observe its real-time behavior. By monitoring system changes, network traffic, and process activities, analysts can identify the malware's functionality and impact. Tools like Cuckoo Sandbox allow for automated dynamic analysis, providing detailed reports on the malware's activities, such as file modifications, registry changes, and connections to external servers. This approach is particularly useful for identifying malicious payloads, persistence mechanisms, and communication patterns.

In addition to static and dynamic analysis, reverse engineering plays a crucial role in understanding complex malware. Using tools like IDA Pro and Ghidra, analysts can decompile and analyze the malware's code to uncover its inner workings. This process requires knowledge of assembly language, debugging techniques, and code structures. Reverse engineering is often necessary for dissecting advanced malware, such as nation-state cyber threats, highly obfuscated ransomware, or zero-day exploits. While time-consuming and technically demanding, it provides the most in-depth understanding of a malware's functionality.

Malware developers implement various anti-analysis techniques to evade detection and hinder analysis efforts. These techniques include code obfuscation, encryption, anti-debugging mechanisms, and sandbox detection. Some malware samples check for virtual environments and terminate execution if they detect signs of an analysis lab. Others use polymorphic or metamorphic techniques to modify their code structure dynamically, making traditional signature-based detection ineffective. Understanding these evasion tactics is crucial for analysts to adapt their methods and bypass malware defenses.

Beyond individual malware samples, malware analysis contributes to broader cybersecurity efforts, such as threat intelligence and incident response. By analyzing malware artifacts, security teams can extract indicators of compromise (IoCs) that help identify and mitigate infections across networks. IoCs include IP addresses, domain names, file hashes, and registry modifications associated with malicious activity. Sharing these findings with the cybersecurity community enhances collective defense efforts against emerging threats.

Organizations leverage malware analysis to strengthen their security posture, improve detection capabilities, and develop countermeasures. Security teams use insights from malware analysis to enhance endpoint protection, fine-tune intrusion detection systems, and educate employees on cybersecurity best practices. As cyber threats become more sophisticated, integrating malware analysis into an organization's cybersecurity strategy is essential for proactive defense.

The field of malware analysis continues to evolve as cybercriminals develop new attack techniques and security researchers devise advanced detection methods. The rise of artificial intelligence and machine learning has introduced new possibilities for automating malware detection and classification. At the same time, adversaries leverage AI to create more evasive threats, resulting in an ongoing battle between attackers and defenders. Continuous learning, collaboration, and research are key to staying ahead in the ever-changing landscape of malware analysis.

Malware analysis is a dynamic and challenging discipline that plays a vital role in cybersecurity. It requires a combination of technical expertise, problem-solving skills, and adaptability to counter the constantly evolving tactics of cybercriminals. Whether through static analysis, dynamic testing, or reverse engineering, malware analysts uncover valuable intelligence that helps protect systems and users from malicious threats. As cyberattacks grow in complexity, the importance of skilled malware analysts will only continue to increase, shaping the future of cybersecurity defense.

History of Malware and Cyber Threats

The history of malware and cyber threats is a fascinating journey that reflects the evolution of computing, the increasing complexity of cyberattacks, and the ongoing battle between attackers and defenders. Malware, short for malicious software, has existed in some form since the early days of computing, and its development has paralleled the growth of the internet and digital technology. From simple experiments to sophisticated nation-state cyberweapons, malware has become one of the most significant threats in modern cybersecurity.

The first known instance of a self-replicating program dates back to the 1970s with the creation of the Creeper virus. Creeper was not designed to be malicious but rather as an experiment in self-propagation. It was developed by Bob Thomas and ran on ARPANET, the predecessor to the modern internet. Creeper would display the message "I'M THE CREEPER: CATCH ME IF YOU CAN" as it moved from one system to another. In response, Ray Tomlinson, the creator of email, developed the first known antivirus program, called Reaper, which was designed to track and delete Creeper. This event marked the beginning of the ongoing battle between malware and security software.

The 1980s saw the emergence of more advanced malware with malicious intent. One of the earliest examples was the Elk Cloner virus, created in 1982 by a 15-year-old programmer named Rich Skrenta. Elk Cloner was designed to infect Apple II computers by spreading through infected floppy disks. Once activated, it would display a humorous message, but its ability to spread across multiple systems demonstrated the potential of malware to disrupt computing environments. During this period, the term "computer virus" was coined by Fred Cohen in his research on self-replicating code. His work laid the foundation for understanding and analyzing malware threats.

By the late 1980s and early 1990s, the rise of personal computers and the expansion of networks led to a surge in malware attacks. The Brain virus, created in 1986 by two Pakistani brothers, is widely recognized as the first PC virus. It was initially designed to protect software from piracy, but it unintentionally spread beyond its intended targets. Around the same time, viruses such as Jerusalem and Cascade became notorious for their destructive effects, including file deletion and system slowdowns. The emergence of the Morris Worm in 1988 was another pivotal moment in cybersecurity history. Designed by Robert Tappan Morris, the worm spread across ARPANET, causing significant disruptions and exposing vulnerabilities in network security.

The 1990s marked the beginning of large-scale cyber threats, driven by the rise of the internet and email communication. The Melissa virus, which appeared in 1999, was among the first to exploit email as a vector for rapid propagation. It spread through infected Microsoft Word documents and overloaded email servers worldwide. Around the same time, macro viruses became increasingly prevalent, exploiting vulnerabilities in office productivity software to execute malicious code. The decade also saw the emergence of Trojan horses, which disguised themselves as legitimate software while secretly performing malicious activities in the background.

The early 2000s witnessed the rise of internet worms that spread at unprecedented speeds. The ILOVEYOU worm, which appeared in 2000, infected millions of computers within hours by tricking users into opening an email attachment disguised as a love letter. It caused billions of dollars in damages by overwriting files and sending copies of itself to email contacts. Other notorious worms, such as Code Red, Nimda, and Blaster, exploited vulnerabilities in Windows operating systems to propagate across networks without user interaction. These incidents highlighted the urgent need for security patches and proactive defense measures.

As cyber threats evolved, cybercriminals began monetizing malware on a large scale. The mid-2000s saw the rise of botnets, networks of infected computers controlled remotely by attackers. These botnets were used for various criminal activities, including distributed denial-of-service (DDoS) attacks, spam distribution, and financial fraud. The Zeus Trojan, which emerged in 2007, became one of the most infamous banking malware threats, stealing millions of dollars from online banking accounts. Around the same time, ransomware attacks started gaining traction, with early variants encrypting victims' files and demanding payments for decryption keys.

The 2010s marked the emergence of nation-state cyber warfare and sophisticated malware campaigns. Stuxnet, discovered in 2010, was one of the most advanced cyber weapons ever developed. Designed to target Iran's nuclear program, it demonstrated how malware could be used for geopolitical objectives, setting a precedent for cyber warfare. Other state-sponsored malware campaigns, such as Flame, Duqu, and APT (Advanced Persistent Threat) attacks, further highlighted the growing role of cyber threats in global security. The decade also saw a significant rise in ransomware attacks, with strains like WannaCry and NotPetya causing widespread disruption across industries.

The modern era of malware is characterized by increasing complexity, automation, and the use of artificial intelligence in both attacks and defense. Cybercriminals now leverage machine learning to create more evasive malware that can bypass traditional security measures. Fileless malware, which operates entirely in memory without leaving traces on disk, has become a major concern for security professionals. Meanwhile, ransomware-as-a-service (RaaS) platforms have made it easier for attackers to launch large-scale extortion campaigns without technical expertise.

As cyber threats continue to evolve, the importance of malware analysis, threat intelligence, and cybersecurity awareness has never been greater. The history of malware serves as a reminder that cyber threats are constantly adapting, requiring continuous innovation in defense strategies. From the early experiments of the Creeper virus to the sophisticated nation-state attacks of today, malware has shaped the cybersecurity landscape, influencing the way organizations and individuals protect themselves in an increasingly digital world.

Types of Malware: An Overview

Malware, short for malicious software, is a broad term that encompasses various types of software designed to infiltrate, damage, or exploit computer systems and networks. Cybercriminals and threat actors use malware for a wide range of malicious purposes, including financial fraud, espionage, data theft, and system disruption. As cybersecurity defenses evolve, so do the techniques and forms of malware, making it crucial for security professionals to understand the different types of threats they may encounter. Each type of malware operates differently, using unique mechanisms to infect, spread, and achieve its objectives.

Viruses are one of the oldest and most well-known forms of malware. A computer virus attaches itself to a legitimate file or program and spreads when the infected file is executed. Viruses can corrupt or delete data, slow down system performance, and, in some cases, make a computer completely inoperable. Unlike other types of malware, viruses require user interaction to propagate, such as opening an infected email attachment or downloading a compromised file. Some of the most notorious viruses in history have caused widespread damage, demonstrating how even simple malicious code can disrupt global computer networks.

Worms, unlike viruses, do not need a host file to spread. They are self-replicating programs that can move from one system to another without any user intervention. Worms often exploit security vulnerabilities in network protocols to spread rapidly across connected devices. Once inside a system, a worm can consume system resources, overload network traffic, and create backdoors for other types of malware. Some worms carry payloads designed to steal information, delete files, or install additional malware. The ability of worms to propagate autonomously makes them particularly dangerous in corporate and enterprise environments, where large networks provide an ideal breeding ground for infection.

Trojans, or Trojan horses, disguise themselves as legitimate software to trick users into executing them. Unlike viruses and worms, Trojans do not replicate themselves, but they often serve as a gateway for other malware. Once executed, a Trojan can create backdoors, allowing attackers to gain unauthorized access to the infected system. Trojans are commonly used for espionage, keylogging, and remote control of compromised devices. Cybercriminals distribute Trojans through fake software downloads, malicious email attachments, and compromised websites. Because they appear harmless, Trojans can bypass many traditional security measures, making them a preferred tool for cybercriminals.

Ransomware is one of the most financially damaging forms of malware. It encrypts the victim's files or locks their entire system, demanding a ransom payment in exchange for the decryption key. Ransomware attacks often target businesses, hospitals, and government institutions, where downtime can result in severe financial and operational consequences. Some ransomware variants employ advanced encryption techniques that make file recovery nearly impossible without the decryption key. Attackers often demand payment in cryptocurrency to remain anonymous. Ransomware has evolved significantly in recent years, with attackers using sophisticated techniques to evade detection and maximize their profits.

Spyware is designed to secretly monitor a user's activities and collect sensitive information without their knowledge. It can record keystrokes, capture screenshots, track browsing habits, and gather personal or financial data. Spyware is often distributed through software bundling, malicious ads, and email attachments. Some spyware variants specifically target banking credentials, login information, and other valuable data that can be sold on the dark web. Governments and organizations have also used spyware for surveillance purposes, raising concerns about privacy and ethical implications. Because spyware operates silently in the background, it can remain undetected for extended periods, making it a persistent threat to users and organizations.

Adware, while not always malicious, can be intrusive and disruptive. It is designed to display unwanted advertisements, often redirecting users to suspicious websites or collecting browsing data for targeted marketing. Some adware variants are harmless, serving only as an annoyance, while others can install additional malware or expose users to phishing attacks. Adware is commonly bundled with free software downloads, tricking users into installing it unintentionally. While some adware can be removed easily, more advanced versions can modify system settings and make removal difficult without specialized security tools.

Rootkits are a particularly stealthy form of malware that provides attackers with deep access to a compromised system. A rootkit can hide its presence from traditional antivirus software, allowing attackers to maintain control over an infected machine for an extended period. Rootkits operate at the kernel level, meaning they can modify system processes, intercept network communications, and disable security mechanisms. Some rootkits are used for espionage, enabling attackers to monitor a victim's activities undetected. Because rootkits can embed themselves deep within the operating system, removing them often requires specialized tools or a complete system reinstallation.

Fileless malware is a modern and sophisticated type of malware that does not rely on traditional files for execution. Instead, it operates entirely in system memory, making it difficult for antivirus programs to detect and remove. Fileless malware often exploits legitimate system processes, such as PowerShell or Windows Management Instrumentation (WMI), to execute malicious code. Because it does not leave a trace on the hard drive, forensic analysis and mitigation become challenging. Attackers use fileless malware for targeted attacks, espionage, and data exfiltration, taking advantage of its stealthy nature to evade security defenses.

Botnets consist of networks of infected computers controlled remotely by cybercriminals. These compromised machines, often referred to as "zombies," can be used for various malicious activities, such as launching distributed denial-of-service (DDoS) attacks, sending spam emails, and spreading additional malware. Botnets are typically created through malware infections that install a command-and-control (C2) module on the victim's system. Once part of a botnet, an infected machine can receive commands from the attacker without the owner's knowledge. Some botnets consist of millions of infected devices, creating a powerful tool for cybercriminals to carry out large-scale attacks.

Malware continues to evolve, with attackers developing new variants that evade detection and exploit emerging technologies. As the cybersecurity landscape changes, understanding the different types of malware is essential for developing effective defense strategies. Whether through viruses, worms, Trojans, ransomware, spyware, or other forms of malware, cyber threats pose a significant risk to individuals and organizations. Security professionals must stay informed about the latest malware trends and continuously adapt their defenses to counter increasingly sophisticated attacks.

Malware Infection Vectors

Malware infection vectors are the various methods and pathways through which malicious software infiltrates computer systems, networks, and devices. Cybercriminals continuously refine and evolve their tactics to exploit vulnerabilities and human behaviors, making infection vectors a crucial aspect of cybersecurity. Understanding how malware spreads is essential for developing effective defense strategies and minimizing risks in both individual and organizational environments. Attackers use multiple techniques to deliver malware, ranging from social engineering and phishing to exploiting software vulnerabilities and leveraging compromised websites.

Email remains one of the most common and effective malware infection vectors. Cybercriminals often craft phishing emails that contain malicious attachments or links to infected websites. These emails may appear to come from legitimate sources, such as banks, government agencies, or well-known companies, tricking recipients into opening the attachments or clicking on the links. Once executed, the malware can install itself on the victim's system, steal sensitive information, or establish persistence for further exploitation. Spear-phishing attacks, which target specific individuals or organizations with highly tailored messages, increase the chances of success by exploiting trust and familiarity.

Drive-by downloads are another major infection vector that takes advantage of vulnerabilities in web browsers and plugins. When users visit a compromised or malicious website, malware can be automatically downloaded and executed without their knowledge. These attacks often exploit security flaws in outdated software, allowing attackers to inject malicious scripts or payloads into legitimate web pages. Drive-by downloads are particularly dangerous because they require no user interaction beyond visiting an infected site. Cybercriminals often use exploit kits to automate the process, scanning a visitor's system for vulnerabilities and deploying malware accordingly.

Removable media, such as USB flash drives and external hard drives, serve as a physical malware infection vector. Attackers can pre-load malware onto USB devices and distribute them in public places, banking on the curiosity of unsuspecting users. Once the USB device is plugged into a system, the malware can automatically execute and spread. Some advanced threats, such as Stuxnet, have demonstrated how malware delivered through USB drives can compromise industrial control systems and cause significant damage. Disabling autorun features and scanning removable media before use are essential measures to mitigate this risk.

Software vulnerabilities provide another common pathway for malware infections. Attackers exploit weaknesses in operating systems, applications, and firmware to execute malicious code. Zero-day vulnerabilities, which are security flaws unknown to vendors and the public, present significant risks because there are no available patches at the time of discovery. Cybercriminals and state-sponsored attackers often use zero-day exploits to infiltrate high-value targets before the vulnerability is publicly disclosed and patched. Keeping software updated and applying security patches promptly are crucial for defending against malware infections that exploit software flaws.

Malicious advertisements, or malvertising, leverage online advertising networks to distribute malware. Attackers inject malicious code into legitimate ad networks, causing infected advertisements to appear on reputable websites. Users who click on these ads may be redirected to malicious websites that deploy malware, or they may be exposed to exploit kits that silently deliver payloads in the background. Since malvertising can appear on well-known websites, users often have no reason to suspect a threat. Ad-blocking software and security-focused browser extensions can help reduce the risk of malvertising-based infections.

Social engineering plays a significant role in malware distribution by manipulating human behavior and trust. Attackers craft convincing scenarios that persuade victims to download and execute malware willingly. This can take the form of fake software updates, fraudulent tech support scams, or deceptive pop-up messages claiming that a system is infected with a virus. Social engineering attacks often bypass traditional security measures because they exploit human psychology rather than technical vulnerabilities. Training users to recognize and avoid suspicious downloads, messages, and requests is a key component of reducing social engineering-based malware infections.

Peer-to-peer (P2P) networks and file-sharing platforms have long been associated with malware infections. Users who download software, movies, or music from untrusted sources risk exposing their systems to malware. Cybercriminals often disguise malicious executables as popular files, tricking users into executing them. Torrent downloads, cracked software, and pirated content are particularly risky, as they frequently contain hidden malware. Some malware variants specifically target P2P users by embedding themselves in shared files and spreading across connected devices. Avoiding unverified downloads and using reputable sources for software and media can help prevent infections from P2P networks.

Compromised websites and watering hole attacks target specific organizations or user groups by infecting websites frequently visited by their intended victims. Attackers identify websites that are likely to attract their targets and inject malicious scripts or backdoors into them. When a visitor accesses the infected website, malware is silently deployed onto their system. This method is particularly effective for targeting industries, government agencies, and corporations with specialized interests. Watering hole attacks are difficult to detect because they exploit trust in familiar websites. Regular security monitoring and endpoint protection can help detect and mitigate these threats.

Mobile devices are increasingly targeted by malware infection vectors, especially through malicious apps and phishing links. Attackers distribute fake apps through third-party app stores, social media links, and fraudulent emails, luring users into installing them. Once installed, these apps can steal personal information, track user activity, or install additional malware. Mobile malware often requests excessive permissions, granting attackers deep access to the device. Official app stores implement security measures to reduce the spread of malicious apps, but users should remain cautious by verifying app legitimacy and permissions before installation.

Remote desktop protocol (RDP) and other remote access technologies have become significant infection vectors, particularly for ransomware and botnet attacks. Cybercriminals exploit weak or improperly configured RDP connections to gain unauthorized access to systems. Once inside, they can deploy malware, exfiltrate sensitive data, or launch large-scale ransomware attacks. Brute-force attacks, credential stuffing, and stolen login credentials are common methods used to compromise RDP access. Implementing strong authentication, using VPNs, and restricting remote access to trusted IPs are critical defenses against RDP-based malware infections.

Cloud services and SaaS platforms present new opportunities for malware distribution. Attackers leverage cloud-based file-sharing services to host and distribute malicious payloads. Users who download files from compromised cloud storage links may unknowingly introduce malware into their organization. Additionally, attackers exploit misconfigured cloud environments to deploy cryptojacking malware, which hijacks computing resources to mine cryptocurrency. As cloud adoption continues to grow, securing cloud storage, implementing access controls, and monitoring for suspicious activities are essential for preventing malware infections through cloud-based attack vectors.

As cyber threats continue to evolve, attackers will find new ways to exploit human behavior, technological vulnerabilities, and emerging digital environments. Understanding malware infection vectors is a crucial step in strengthening cybersecurity defenses and reducing the risk of malware infiltrating systems. Organizations and individuals must remain vigilant by adopting security best practices, keeping software up to date, and educating users on the latest threats to mitigate the ever-growing landscape of malware infections.

Basic Dynamic Analysis Techniques

Dynamic analysis is a crucial approach in malware analysis that involves executing malicious software in a controlled environment to observe its behavior. Unlike static analysis, which focuses on inspecting the malware's code without running it, dynamic analysis provides real-time insights into how the malware interacts with the system. By monitoring file system changes, registry modifications, network connections, and process activities, analysts can determine the malware's impact, identify potential indicators of compromise, and develop effective countermeasures. Basic dynamic analysis techniques are essential for security researchers, incident responders, and malware analysts who need to quickly assess threats without diving into complex reverse engineering.

The first step in dynamic analysis is setting up a controlled environment to safely execute the malware. Analysts typically use virtual machines (VMs) or sandbox environments to isolate the malware and prevent accidental infections. Virtualization tools like VMware, VirtualBox, and Hyper-V allow researchers to create isolated instances of operating systems where malware can be executed without affecting the host machine. Sandboxes such as Cuckoo Sandbox provide automated analysis by executing the malware and generating detailed reports on its behavior. Before running the malware, analysts take a baseline snapshot of the system, which allows them to compare pre- and post-infection states to identify changes introduced by the malware.

Process monitoring is a fundamental technique in dynamic analysis, as it reveals how the malware interacts with the operating system and other applications. Tools like Process Explorer and Process Monitor from Sysinternals help analysts track newly spawned processes, detect unusual activity, and observe how the malware modifies system resources. When malware executes, it often creates child processes, injects code into legitimate applications, or terminates security-related processes to evade detection. By analyzing process activity, analysts can determine whether the malware exhibits behaviors such as persistence mechanisms, privilege escalation, or attempts to disable security software.

File system monitoring is another essential aspect of dynamic analysis. Malware often creates, modifies, or deletes files as part of its execution. Some threats drop additional payloads, modify configuration files, or overwrite system components to maintain persistence. Tools like ProcMon and FileMon help analysts track file system modifications in real time. By examining file creation events and identifying suspicious file paths, analysts can uncover hidden malware components and determine how the malware spreads within the system. Some malware families create encrypted or obfuscated files to store stolen data or configuration settings, making file system analysis a valuable technique for uncovering hidden threats.

Registry monitoring is particularly important when analyzing Windows-based malware, as many threats modify registry keys to establish persistence. The Windows Registry contains critical configuration settings, and malware often uses it to ensure execution upon system reboot. Malware may add entries to the "Run" or "RunOnce" keys, modify existing configurations, or disable security features. Tools like Regshot allow analysts to take registry snapshots before and after malware execution, highlighting any changes made by the malware. Understanding registry modifications helps analysts determine how the malware maintains access to the system and whether it attempts to manipulate security settings or disable defenses.

Network activity monitoring provides valuable insights into how malware communicates with external systems. Many threats rely on command-and-control (C2) servers to receive instructions, exfiltrate stolen data, or download additional payloads. Tools like Wireshark and Fiddler allow analysts to capture network traffic and analyze communication patterns. By monitoring network requests, analysts can identify malicious domain names, IP addresses, and data transmission methods used by the malware. Some malware attempts to evade detection by encrypting its network traffic, using domain generation algorithms (DGA) to create random URLs, or utilizing protocols like DNS tunneling to bypass traditional security controls. Identifying and blocking these network indicators can help prevent further infections and mitigate damage.

Behavioral analysis focuses on understanding how the malware interacts with the system and whether it exhibits evasive techniques.

Some malware samples detect virtual environments and refuse to execute if they detect sandboxing tools or debugging software. Malware authors implement anti-analysis techniques such as delaying execution, checking for debugger presence, or verifying the presence of monitoring tools. To counteract these techniques, analysts may use tools like FakeNet to simulate network responses or employ anti-anti-analysis techniques to deceive the malware into running normally. By studying how malware behaves under different conditions, analysts can extract valuable intelligence on its purpose and intent.

Memory analysis plays a critical role in dynamic malware analysis, especially when dealing with fileless malware that operates entirely in RAM. Traditional antivirus solutions may fail to detect fileless malware because it does not leave traces on disk. Tools like Volatility and RAM capture utilities allow analysts to extract and analyze memory contents to uncover hidden processes, injected code, and decryption keys. By examining memory structures, analysts can reconstruct executable code, identify active malware threads, and determine how the malware manipulates system memory. Memory forensics is particularly useful for analyzing advanced persistent threats (APTs) and sophisticated malware that employs stealth techniques.

Executing malware in a controlled environment carries inherent risks, so analysts must take precautions to minimize potential damage. Using snapshots and reverting to clean states ensures that malware infections do not persist beyond analysis sessions. Disabling network connectivity or redirecting traffic through controlled environments prevents malware from communicating with external C2 servers. Implementing logging and monitoring solutions helps analysts capture critical events for further investigation. When dealing with highly destructive malware, analysts may use specialized air-gapped environments to prevent unintended spread. Proper isolation and security measures are crucial for conducting dynamic analysis safely.

Basic dynamic analysis techniques provide a structured approach to understanding malware behavior without requiring deep knowledge of reverse engineering. By monitoring processes, file system changes, registry modifications, network activity, and memory interactions, analysts can gather valuable intelligence on how malware operates. These insights help security teams develop detection signatures, improve threat hunting capabilities, and implement defensive measures to mitigate malware threats. As cyber threats continue to evolve, dynamic analysis remains a fundamental component of modern cybersecurity, enabling researchers to stay ahead of attackers and protect systems from emerging malware strains.

Advanced Static Analysis: Reverse Engineering

Reverse engineering is a critical skill in malware analysis that allows security researchers to deconstruct malicious software and understand its inner workings. Unlike dynamic analysis, which involves executing malware to observe its behavior, advanced static analysis focuses on dissecting the code without running it. This approach is essential when dealing with highly evasive malware that detects sandboxes, encrypted payloads, or fileless execution methods. By using disassemblers, decompilers, and debugging tools, analysts can examine the malware's instructions, identify obfuscation techniques, and extract valuable intelligence about its functionality, persistence mechanisms, and command-and-control (C2) infrastructure.

One of the first steps in reverse engineering malware is to examine its binary structure. Portable Executable (PE) files in Windows and Executable and Linkable Format (ELF) files in Linux contain important metadata that provides insight into the malware's architecture, dependencies, and execution flow. Tools like PEStudio and readelf allow analysts to inspect headers, imported functions, and section structures. By analyzing the import table, researchers can determine which system libraries the malware relies on, such as network-related APIs, file manipulation functions, or registry modification routines. Identifying these dependencies helps analysts infer the malware's capabilities, such as whether it can establish persistence, steal credentials, or exfiltrate data.

Disassembly is a core technique in advanced static analysis, transforming compiled binary code into human-readable assembly instructions. Tools like IDA Pro, Ghidra, and Radare2 allow analysts to decompile malware and trace its execution path. Assembly language, while complex, provides an accurate representation of how the malware interacts with the system. Analysts can identify key functions, analyze branching logic, and track data flow through registers and memory locations. Control flow analysis helps determine how different parts of the malware are connected, revealing obfuscated routines or hidden functionality. Some malware samples employ anti-disassembly techniques, such as inserting junk code, breaking instruction alignment, or using opaque predicates to mislead reverse engineers.

Obfuscation and encryption are common techniques used by malware authors to hinder analysis. Many threats employ packers and cryptors to modify their code structure and evade signature-based detection. Unpacking the malware is often necessary before meaningful analysis can begin. Analysts use tools like UPX for detecting standard packers and custom scripts for unpacking more complex obfuscation layers. In cases where the malware decrypts itself during execution, a debugger like x64dbg or OllyDbg can help analysts set breakpoints, dump memory regions, and extract decrypted payloads. Understanding how malware conceals its true intent is crucial for reconstructing its execution logic and detecting similar threats.

String analysis is another valuable technique in static reverse engineering. Malware binaries often contain embedded strings that reveal useful information, such as hardcoded URLs, registry keys, decryption keys, or error messages. Tools like Strings, Binwalk, and Floss help extract plaintext and encoded strings from binaries. Many modern malware samples use string encryption or obfuscation techniques to hide indicators of compromise. Analysts must trace the decryption routines within the code to reconstruct meaningful strings dynamically. Identifying hardcoded credentials, C2 server addresses, or infection markers allows security teams to develop detection rules and block malicious infrastructure.

Function analysis helps determine the purpose of different code segments within the malware. By examining API calls and function arguments, analysts can infer whether the malware is designed for keylogging, screen capturing, file encryption, or privilege escalation. Reversing function logic requires stepping through disassembled code, identifying loops, conditionals, and memory accesses. Some malware samples include embedded interpreters or execute shellcode dynamically, requiring deeper inspection. Naming functions based on their behavior within IDA Pro or Ghidra improves readability and assists in reconstructing the malware's operational flow. Cross-referencing functions with known malware families can help identify variants and improve attribution efforts.

Malware often incorporates anti-analysis techniques to prevent or slow down reverse engineering. These methods include anti-debugging, anti-virtualization, and anti-emulation strategies. Anti-debugging techniques involve checking for running debuggers, setting hardware breakpoints, or manipulating system calls to disrupt analysis tools. Malware may detect virtualized environments by querying specific registry keys, checking for VM-related drivers, or measuring execution timing anomalies. Advanced threats even use hardware-assisted techniques, such as Intel VT-x detection, to evade analysis in sandbox environments. Reverse engineers counteract these techniques by patching binaries, modifying memory at runtime, or using stealth debugging tools to bypass detection checks.

Reversing polymorphic and metamorphic malware presents additional challenges. Polymorphic malware dynamically alters its code structure during execution, making traditional signature-based detection ineffective. It uses encryption wrappers, random instruction insertion, and register swaps to generate unique variations of itself. Metamorphic malware goes a step further by completely rewriting its code with each new infection, ensuring that no two samples are identical. To analyze such threats, researchers must focus on behavioral patterns, opcode sequences, and entropy measurements rather than relying on static signatures. Identifying common decryption loops, unpacking stages, or self-modifying code segments provides a pathway to understanding these complex threats.

Extracting indicators of compromise (IoCs) is a critical outcome of reverse engineering. Once analysts determine how the malware operates, they document key findings such as file hashes, network signatures, mutex values, registry modifications, and injected process names. These IoCs help security teams detect and mitigate infections before they spread. Reverse engineers also contribute to signature-based detection methods, writing YARA rules to identify malware families across multiple environments. Sharing IoCs with threat intelligence platforms enhances collective defense efforts, enabling organizations to block emerging threats more effectively.

Reverse engineering is an advanced discipline that requires a deep understanding of assembly language, system internals, and malware behaviors. The complexity of modern threats demands continuous learning and adaptation. By leveraging tools like IDA Pro, Ghidra, and dynamic debugging frameworks, analysts can dismantle even the most sophisticated malware samples. Whether uncovering hidden payloads, decrypting embedded strings, or bypassing anti-analysis mechanisms, reverse engineering provides invaluable insights into how malware functions. Mastering this skill enables security professionals to defend against evolving cyber threats, mitigate large-scale attacks, and improve global cybersecurity resilience.

Advanced Dynamic Analysis: Debugging Malware

Debugging is a critical component of advanced dynamic malware analysis that allows researchers to examine malicious software in real-time as it executes. Unlike basic dynamic analysis, which involves passive observation of a malware sample's behavior using monitoring tools, debugging enables analysts to step through the malware's code, modify registers, inspect memory, and analyze runtime changes. This hands-on approach is particularly useful for understanding complex malware, unpacking obfuscated payloads, bypassing anti-analysis techniques, and identifying hidden functionalities that might not be apparent through static or automated analysis. By using debuggers such as x64dbg, OllyDbg, and WinDbg, analysts can manipulate the execution flow of malware, extract critical data, and determine how it interacts with the operating system.

The first step in debugging malware is setting up a secure and controlled environment. Since debugging involves executing the malware, precautions must be taken to prevent accidental infections or network propagation. Analysts typically use isolated virtual machines (VMs) with snapshot capabilities to revert the system to a clean state after analysis. Tools such as VMware and VirtualBox allow for flexible VM configurations with restricted network access to prevent communication with external command-and-control (C2) servers. Some malware samples attempt to detect virtualized environments, so additional measures, such as using hardware-assisted virtualization or modifying VM identifiers, may be necessary to prevent the malware from terminating prematurely.

Once the environment is configured, the malware sample is loaded into a debugger. Debugging begins by analyzing the malware's entry point, where execution starts within the binary. Setting breakpoints at critical functions, such as CreateProcess, WriteFile, or InternetConnect, allows analysts to pause execution at key moments and inspect the malware's actions. By stepping through the code instruction by instruction, analysts can observe how the malware manipulates system resources, decrypts payloads, or establishes persistence. This level of control provides deep insights into the malware's behavior and can reveal its true intentions, even if it employs obfuscation techniques to hide its functionality.

Many malware samples use packing or encryption techniques to conceal their payloads and evade detection. Packed malware often extracts and executes its real code at runtime, making static analysis ineffective. Debugging allows analysts to bypass these protections by identifying and dumping the unpacked code from memory. By placing breakpoints on key Windows API calls like VirtualAlloc, NtUnmapViewOfSection, or WriteProcessMemory, analysts can detect when the malware loads additional data into memory. Once the unpacked payload is located, it can be extracted using memory-dumping tools like Scylla or PE-sieve, allowing analysts to examine the true executable file without its protective wrapper.

Malware authors frequently implement anti-debugging techniques to detect and disrupt debugging efforts. These techniques include checking for attached debuggers, detecting breakpoints, modifying debugging structures, and using timing-based evasion methods. Common anti-debugging functions, such as IsDebuggerPresent and CheckRemoteDebuggerPresent, allow malware to identify if it is running under a debugger. More advanced techniques involve manipulating the NtGlobalFlag or BeingDebugged fields in the Process Environment Block (PEB) to disrupt debugging attempts. Analysts can counter these tactics by patching relevant instructions, modifying memory values, or using plugins that automatically bypass common anti-debugging checks.

Code injection and process hollowing are techniques used by malware to execute within legitimate system processes, making detection more difficult. Debugging is an effective way to analyze these methods by tracing process creation events and injected code execution. By monitoring API calls like OpenProcess, VirtualAllocEx, WriteProcessMemory, and CreateRemoteThread, analysts can determine where and how the malware injects its code. Once identified, the injected payload can be extracted and analyzed separately to understand its purpose. Debugging also helps in detecting reflective DLL injection, where malware loads a malicious DLL into memory without touching the disk, making traditional antivirus detection ineffective.

Some malware relies on environment checks to avoid running in an analysis environment. These checks include detecting sandbox indicators, querying hardware properties, checking for specific registry keys, or performing system uptime calculations. Malware may also attempt to detect debuggers by executing instructions such as INT 3, RDTSCP, or RDTSC, which measure execution timing to identify unnatural delays caused by breakpoints. Analysts can bypass these checks by modifying system responses, adjusting CPU timing values, or patching conditional jumps that prevent execution in debugging environments. By controlling how the malware perceives its surroundings, analysts can force it to reveal its full behavior.

Network communication is a vital aspect of many malware samples, as they often rely on external servers for instructions, data exfiltration, or downloading additional payloads. Debugging allows analysts to manipulate network traffic by intercepting function calls related to network operations. By setting breakpoints on API calls like send, recv, WinHttpConnect, or InternetOpenUrl, analysts can capture and modify network requests in real-time. This technique helps in extracting command-and-control URLs, deobfuscating encryption routines, and redirecting malicious traffic to controlled environments for further study. Some malware uses domain generation algorithms (DGA) to create randomized C2 server addresses dynamically, and debugging provides a way to reverse-engineer these algorithms for proactive defense.

Ransomware analysis benefits greatly from debugging, as it enables analysts to extract encryption keys, identify weaknesses in the encryption process, and potentially develop decryption tools. By tracing the ransomware's execution flow, analysts can determine how it interacts with files, what encryption libraries it uses, and whether it leaves any recoverable artifacts in memory. Some ransomware variants implement secure encryption methods, making decryption impossible without the attacker's private key. However, debugging can sometimes reveal flaws in key generation, allowing security researchers to develop decryptors for victims.

Advanced debugging also plays a crucial role in detecting rootkits, which operate at the kernel level and manipulate system components to hide their presence. Kernel-mode debugging requires specialized tools such as WinDbg and a dedicated debugging system to analyze low-level interactions between malware and the operating system. By stepping through kernel routines, analysts can detect unauthorized modifications to system drivers, identify hidden processes, and uncover techniques used by rootkits to intercept system calls. Debugging at this level requires a deep understanding of operating system internals, making it a highly specialized but valuable skill in malware analysis.

Debugging is an essential tool for uncovering the full capabilities of malware, bypassing obfuscation techniques, and extracting valuable threat intelligence. By carefully controlling the execution flow, modifying system responses, and analyzing runtime behavior, analysts can gain deep insights into how malware operates and how to develop effective countermeasures. Mastering debugging techniques requires patience, experience, and a strong understanding of system internals, but it remains one of the most powerful methods for analyzing and mitigating modern cyber threats.

Behavioral Analysis of Malware

Behavioral analysis of malware is a crucial technique used to understand how malicious software interacts with a system in real-time. Unlike static analysis, which involves examining the malware's code without executing it, behavioral analysis focuses on observing the malware's actions when it runs in a controlled environment. This approach allows analysts to identify its capabilities, persistence mechanisms, network communications, and potential impact on an infected system. By monitoring system changes, network activity, and process execution, analysts can extract valuable indicators of compromise (IoCs) and develop effective detection and mitigation strategies.

One of the primary goals of behavioral analysis is to determine how malware executes and what modifications it makes to the host system. Malware can create new files, modify existing ones, inject itself into running processes, or establish persistence by altering registry keys. By using tools such as Process Monitor and Sysinternals Suite, analysts can track file system changes in real-time. Some malware variants drop additional payloads, create hidden directories, or modify system files to maintain control over the system. Understanding these behaviors helps security teams implement protective measures to prevent reinfection.

Process execution analysis is another critical aspect of behavioral analysis. When malware runs, it may spawn new processes, inject code into legitimate applications, or manipulate system processes to conceal its presence. Tools like Process Explorer allow analysts to examine running processes, detect suspicious activity, and identify unauthorized modifications. Some malware terminates security-related processes to disable antivirus software or firewalls. By monitoring process creation and termination events, analysts can determine whether the malware employs stealth techniques, such as process hollowing or thread injection, to evade detection.

Registry modifications are a common tactic used by malware to ensure persistence on an infected system. Windows-based malware often creates or modifies registry keys to execute automatically upon system startup. The "Run" and "RunOnce" registry keys are frequently targeted to maintain persistence. By using registry monitoring tools like Regshot, analysts can compare system snapshots before and after malware execution to identify registry changes. Some advanced malware encrypts or obfuscates its registry entries to evade detection, requiring additional analysis to uncover its persistence mechanisms.

Network activity analysis provides insight into how malware communicates with external servers. Many malware variants rely on command-and-control (C2) servers to receive instructions, exfiltrate data, or download additional payloads. By capturing and analyzing network traffic using tools like Wireshark and Fiddler, analysts can identify suspicious IP addresses, domains, and protocols used by the malware. Some malware employs domain generation algorithms (DGA) to create dynamic C2 addresses, making traditional blacklisting ineffective. Behavioral analysis helps detect these patterns, enabling security teams to block malicious traffic and disrupt the malware's operations.

Some malware variants use encrypted communications to evade detection. They may employ SSL/TLS encryption, custom obfuscation techniques, or covert channels such as DNS tunneling to exfiltrate data. Network monitoring tools can help analysts identify unusual traffic patterns, detect encryption keys in memory, and reverse-engineer the malware's communication protocols. In some cases, decrypting network traffic provides valuable information about the attacker's infrastructure, revealing additional IoCs that can be used for threat hunting and mitigation.

Behavioral analysis also helps identify user interaction dependencies. Some malware requires user actions to trigger execution, such as opening a malicious email attachment, clicking a deceptive link, or enabling macros in an infected document. Analysts simulate these interactions in a controlled environment to determine how the malware spreads and activates. Some sophisticated threats employ social engineering techniques to trick users into bypassing security measures, such as disabling antivirus software or enabling administrative privileges. Understanding these behaviors allows security teams to educate users and implement preventive measures.

Some malware samples detect whether they are running in an analysis environment and alter their behavior accordingly. These anti-analysis techniques include checking for virtual machines, querying hardware configurations, detecting debugging tools, and monitoring execution delays. Malware may terminate itself if it detects sandboxing or attempt to execute only under specific conditions, such as when a real user is actively interacting with the system. Analysts counter these evasion techniques by modifying system properties, using stealth debugging methods, and employing behavioral triggers to coax the malware into revealing its true functionality.

Sandboxing is a powerful tool in behavioral analysis that allows analysts to safely execute and observe malware in an isolated environment. Automated sandbox solutions like Cuckoo Sandbox provide detailed reports on malware behavior, including file system changes, network activity, and registry modifications. These environments mimic real-world systems while preventing the malware from escaping or causing harm. Some malware samples, however, include sandbox detection techniques, requiring analysts to customize the sandbox environment to avoid triggering defensive mechanisms.

Understanding how malware behaves under different conditions provides valuable insights into its purpose and impact. Some malware variants adapt their behavior based on system configurations, geographic locations, or active security measures. For example, certain banking Trojans remain dormant until the user visits a financial website, while ransomware variants may scan for specific file types before initiating encryption. By testing malware in various configurations, analysts can identify hidden functionalities and develop targeted countermeasures.

Behavioral analysis plays a crucial role in detecting fileless malware, which operates entirely in memory without leaving traces on disk. Traditional signature-based detection methods struggle to identify such threats, making behavioral monitoring essential. Fileless malware often abuses legitimate system tools like PowerShell, Windows Management Instrumentation (WMI), or macros to execute malicious payloads. Analysts use memory analysis tools to detect anomalies, track process injections, and uncover hidden scripts that execute in the background.

By thoroughly analyzing malware behavior, security teams can develop proactive defense strategies, improve detection capabilities, and strengthen incident response processes. Behavioral analysis not only helps in understanding how malware operates but also aids in identifying trends in cyber threats. The insights gained from behavioral monitoring allow organizations to enhance security policies, implement effective mitigation techniques, and protect against evolving cyber threats.

Identifying Malware Persistence Mechanisms

Malware persistence is one of the most critical aspects of modern cyber threats. Once malicious software infects a system, it often attempts to establish persistence to survive reboots, user logouts, and security interventions. Without persistence mechanisms, most malware would be removed once the system restarts or an antivirus scan cleans the infected files. Understanding how malware achieves persistence is essential for security analysts and incident responders, as it helps in detecting and removing threats effectively. Different types of malware use various persistence techniques, exploiting system vulnerabilities, built-in features, and user behaviors to maintain control over a compromised environment.

One of the most common persistence methods used by Windows-based malware is registry modification. The Windows Registry is a database that stores configuration settings and system information. Malware frequently creates or alters registry keys to execute itself every time the system starts. The "Run" and "RunOnce" registry keys in HKEY_LOCAL_MACHINE and HKEY_CURRENT_USER are primary targets, as they allow programs to launch automatically upon user login. More advanced malware modifies deeper registry settings, such as adding entries under HKEY_LOCAL_MACHINE\SYSTEM\CurrentControlSet\Services, which allows it to run as a system service. Some threats encrypt or obfuscate their registry values to evade detection, making it more challenging for analysts to identify their presence.

Scheduled tasks provide another effective persistence mechanism. Windows Task Scheduler allows users to automate program execution at specific intervals or events. Malware takes advantage of this feature by creating scheduled tasks that ensure it runs repeatedly, even after reboots. Attackers configure these tasks to execute at startup, on user login, or after a specified delay to avoid immediate detection. Some malware variants use PowerShell scripts embedded in scheduled tasks to download and execute additional payloads dynamically. Since scheduled tasks are a legitimate system feature, they often bypass traditional antivirus detection, making them a popular choice for attackers seeking stealthy persistence.

System services are another method used by malware to maintain persistence. Windows services are background processes that run independently of user sessions. Malware that operates as a service gains the ability to execute with system-level privileges, providing it with greater control and persistence. Attackers create new malicious services or hijack existing ones by modifying their binary paths in the registry. Some malware variants register themselves as legitimate-looking services with misleading names to blend in with normal system processes. Others modify legitimate service executables by injecting malicious code, making detection even more difficult.

Bootkits and rootkits represent some of the most persistent forms of malware. These threats operate at the lowest levels of the system, often modifying the bootloader or kernel components to gain control before the operating system fully loads. Bootkits infect the Master Boot Record (MBR) or EFI partition, ensuring that the malware executes before the operating system starts. Rootkits, on the other hand, operate at the kernel level, intercepting system calls and hiding malicious activity from security tools. Because these techniques compromise the fundamental integrity of the operating system, removing bootkits and rootkits often requires specialized forensic tools or a complete system reinstallation.

DLL hijacking is another technique used by malware to persist within a system. Many Windows applications load Dynamic Link Libraries (DLLs) to function correctly. If an attacker places a malicious DLL in a location where the operating system prioritizes it over legitimate versions, the malware can execute whenever the target application runs. Some malware takes advantage of missing or incorrectly referenced DLL files, tricking programs into loading the malicious library instead. Since the malware operates within the context of a trusted application, it often evades detection by traditional security solutions.

Process injection techniques such as process hollowing and reflective DLL injection also play a role in malware persistence. Process hollowing involves creating a new legitimate process and replacing its memory space with malicious code. This allows the malware to execute under the name of a trusted application, making it harder to detect. Reflective DLL injection, on the other hand, enables malware to load a DLL directly into memory without writing it to disk, reducing its footprint and avoiding signature-based detection. These techniques are often used in conjunction with other persistence mechanisms to maintain long-term control over a system.

Web browser extensions have become a growing target for malware persistence, particularly in attacks aimed at stealing credentials, injecting advertisements, or redirecting users to malicious websites. Malicious extensions disguise themselves as useful add-ons while secretly modifying browser settings, capturing user input, or establishing communication with command-and-control servers.

Since browser extensions operate within the context of the browser rather than the underlying operating system, they often evade traditional endpoint security measures. Some malware families modify browser startup parameters or proxy settings to ensure that their extensions are always loaded, even if the user tries to remove them.

Malware can also persist through Group Policy Objects (GPOs) in enterprise environments. Attackers who gain administrative access to a network can modify GPOs to push malicious scripts or executables to multiple machines. This method is particularly dangerous because it allows malware to spread rapidly across an organization while remaining difficult to remove. Since GPOs are used for legitimate administrative purposes, security teams may overlook modifications that introduce persistent malware into the environment. Monitoring GPO changes and implementing strict access controls are essential to preventing malware from exploiting this technique.

Cloud-based persistence is becoming more common as organizations migrate to cloud environments. Malware targeting cloud platforms often abuses API keys, OAuth tokens, or misconfigured access permissions to maintain persistent access. Attackers may create rogue cloud instances, modify storage permissions, or inject malicious scripts into cloud-based applications. Since cloud infrastructure is designed for scalability and automation, attackers leverage these features to deploy malware that remains active even after initial infections are cleaned. Securing cloud environments requires monitoring for unauthorized API activity, enforcing strict authentication controls, and regularly auditing user permissions.

Persistence techniques continue to evolve as malware authors develop new ways to maintain control over infected systems. Identifying these mechanisms requires a deep understanding of how operating systems function, how legitimate system features can be abused, and how malware adapts to security measures. Security analysts use behavioral analysis, forensic tools, and heuristic detection methods to uncover hidden persistence techniques and remove malware effectively. By understanding how malware establishes and maintains persistence, organizations can implement stronger defenses, reduce the risk of long-term infections, and enhance overall cybersecurity resilience.

Anti-Analysis Techniques Used by Malware

Malware authors constantly develop techniques to evade detection and hinder analysis efforts by security researchers. These anti-analysis techniques are designed to make it difficult for analysts to reverse-engineer, debug, or monitor the malware's behavior. By detecting the presence of analysis tools, virtualized environments, or debugging attempts, malware can alter its execution, terminate itself, or introduce deceptive behaviors that mislead analysts. Understanding these anti-analysis techniques is crucial for cybersecurity professionals to bypass these defenses and accurately assess the capabilities and intent of a malware sample.

One of the most common anti-analysis techniques used by malware is virtual machine (VM) detection. Many security researchers use virtual environments such as VMware, VirtualBox, and Hyper-V to analyze malware safely. Malware can detect these environments by querying specific registry keys, checking for virtualization-related processes, or looking for hardware artifacts unique to virtual machines. Some malware samples inspect the MAC address of the network adapter, as virtual machines often use manufacturer-specific address ranges. If the malware detects that it is running in a VM, it may terminate itself or exhibit benign behavior to avoid detection. Analysts can counter this by modifying VM settings, using custom network adapters, or employing stealth virtualization techniques.

Another widely used evasion tactic is sandbox detection. Automated sandboxes, such as Cuckoo Sandbox, provide a controlled environment where malware is executed and analyzed. Malware authors implement various techniques to identify these environments and prevent execution. One method involves checking system uptime, as sandbox environments often have a short uptime duration. If the malware detects that the system has been running for only a few minutes, it may delay execution to outlast the sandbox's observation period. Some malware samples look for the presence of monitoring tools or hook detection, which sandboxes use to capture malware activity. Analysts can bypass these checks by extending system uptime artificially or modifying sandbox fingerprints to appear like a real user system.

Anti-debugging techniques are another category of anti-analysis methods used to prevent security researchers from stepping through the malware's code using debuggers like x64dbg, OllyDbg, or WinDbg. Malware often calls the Windows API function IsDebuggerPresent to check whether a debugger is attached. If a debugger is detected, the malware may terminate itself or execute misleading instructions. More advanced techniques involve modifying the Process Environment Block (PEB) structure to check the BeingDebugged flag. Some malware manipulates exception handling routines by setting breakpoints on critical instructions, causing debuggers to crash or behave unpredictably. Analysts can bypass these techniques by modifying memory values, patching API calls, or using stealth debugging plugins that hide debugger presence.

Code obfuscation is another powerful anti-analysis strategy that makes malware difficult to read and understand. Malware authors use various obfuscation methods, such as instruction substitution, junk code insertion, and control flow flattening, to disguise the true purpose of their code. Some malware samples use string encryption to hide API calls, file paths, or C2 server addresses. Instead of storing readable strings in the binary, the malware dynamically decrypts them during execution. Analysts must use dynamic analysis techniques such as memory dumping or breakpoints to extract the decrypted strings and uncover the malware's functionality.

Packing is another technique used to evade detection and hinder static analysis. A packer compresses or encrypts the malware's code, making it appear as an unreadable blob to traditional analysis tools. When executed, the malware decompresses or decrypts itself in memory before running its actual payload. Common packers include UPX, Themida, and custom-built packers designed for specific malware families. Analysts can identify packed malware by inspecting entropy levels or using unpacking tools to retrieve the original executable. Debugging the unpacking routine and extracting the decrypted payload is often necessary for further analysis.

Some malware employs anti-memory forensics techniques to prevent analysts from extracting useful information from memory dumps. Fileless malware, for example, operates entirely in memory and never writes malicious components to disk, making traditional antivirus solutions ineffective. Malware may also allocate and encrypt its code in memory, decrypting it only when needed. To counter this, analysts use memory forensic tools like Volatility to capture and analyze process memory, revealing hidden malware components that would otherwise remain undetected.

Timing-based evasion techniques are another sophisticated method used by malware to detect analysis environments. Malware can measure execution delays using high-resolution timers such as QueryPerformanceCounter or RDTSC. Since debuggers and sandboxes introduce slight execution delays due to monitoring overhead, the malware can detect these anomalies and alter its behavior accordingly. Some samples use sleep obfuscation, where the malware introduces long sleep intervals to avoid sandbox execution time limits. Analysts can bypass these techniques by modifying system timers, patching sleep functions, or accelerating execution speeds in controlled environments.

API hammering is an advanced anti-analysis technique where malware floods system logs and monitoring tools with excessive API calls to obscure its real behavior. By making thousands of benign API calls alongside a few critical malicious ones, the malware creates noise that makes analysis difficult. This technique is often used to overwhelm sandboxes and forensic tools, making it harder to extract meaningful insights. Analysts counteract this by filtering out repetitive or irrelevant API calls and focusing on unique system modifications or suspicious behavior.

Some malware samples employ polymorphic or metamorphic techniques to continuously modify their code, making them difficult to detect using traditional signature-based approaches. Polymorphic malware encrypts its payload differently each time it infects a new system, while metamorphic malware rewrites its code structure to appear as an entirely different executable. These techniques make static analysis ineffective, as there is no consistent pattern for detection. Analysts use heuristic and behavior-based detection methods to identify such malware by focusing on functional similarities rather than static signatures.

Encrypted communication is another method malware uses to evade detection. Instead of sending plain-text data over the network, malware encrypts its communication using protocols like SSL/TLS, custom encryption schemes, or steganography. This prevents network monitoring tools from easily capturing command-and-control (C2) communications. Some malware uses domain generation algorithms (DGA) to dynamically create new C2 server addresses, making blacklisting difficult. Analysts use network traffic analysis tools to identify encrypted connections, extract cryptographic keys from memory, or reverse-engineer DGA logic to predict future malicious domains.

Anti-analysis techniques continue to evolve as malware authors develop new ways to bypass security measures. Cybercriminals constantly refine their evasion strategies to stay ahead of detection mechanisms, making it essential for security researchers to adapt and counteract these methods. By understanding and anticipating these anti-analysis techniques, analysts can develop more effective methods for bypassing malware defenses, improving detection rates, and enhancing cybersecurity resilience.

Unpacking Obfuscated Malware

Malware authors frequently use obfuscation techniques to conceal their code and evade detection. One of the most common forms of obfuscation is packing, where the malware's payload is compressed, encrypted, or encoded in such a way that it appears as unreadable data when inspected statically. The goal of packing is to prevent security researchers and automated detection systems from analyzing the malware's true behavior. When executed, the packed malware decrypts or decompresses itself in memory and then executes its real malicious payload. Unpacking obfuscated malware is a crucial skill for malware analysts, as it allows them to extract and analyze the original code hidden within the packed executable.

Packed malware often appears as a small, heavily obfuscated binary with high entropy, indicating that the code is compressed or encrypted. One of the first steps in unpacking malware is identifying the packer used. Common packers such as UPX, Themida, VMProtect, and custom cryptors are widely used to hide malicious payloads. Analysts can use tools like PEiD or Exeinfo PE to determine whether an executable is packed and which packer was used. If the malware is packed with a known packer, it may be possible to use an automated unpacker, such as UPX for UPX-packed files. However, many malware authors modify or stack multiple packing layers to complicate automated unpacking, requiring manual intervention.

Dynamic analysis plays a critical role in unpacking obfuscated malware. Since packed malware extracts itself in memory at runtime, one approach to unpacking is to let the malware execute in a controlled environment and capture the moment when it reveals its true code. Analysts typically use a debugger such as x64dbg or OllyDbg to monitor the execution flow of the packed malware. By setting breakpoints on functions like VirtualAlloc, WriteProcessMemory, or NtUnmapViewOfSection, analysts can detect when the malware writes its unpacked payload into memory. Once the unpacked payload is identified, analysts can dump it from memory using tools like Scylla or Process Hacker, reconstructing the original executable for further analysis.

Another method of unpacking malware involves manually stepping through its execution to locate the unpacking stub, which is the initial part of the code responsible for decrypting or decompressing the payload. The unpacking stub typically uses loops, XOR operations, or API calls to gradually reconstruct the original binary in memory. Analysts can set breakpoints on common API calls used in unpacking routines, such as VirtualProtect, NtAllocateVirtualMemory, or CreateProcessInternalW, and observe how the malware modifies memory regions. By identifying the point where the unpacking stub completes its process, analysts can extract the fully unpacked payload before it executes malicious operations.

Many modern malware variants employ anti-analysis techniques to detect debugging attempts and prevent researchers from unpacking their code. Some packed malware samples check for the presence of debuggers by calling IsDebuggerPresent or inspecting the Process Environment Block (PEB) structure. If debugging is detected, the malware may terminate execution, corrupt its unpacked payload, or enter an infinite loop to frustrate analysis. To bypass these defenses, analysts use anti-anti-debugging techniques such as modifying memory structures, patching anti-debugging checks, or using stealth debugging plugins to avoid detection.

Self-modifying code is another challenge encountered when unpacking malware. Some packers modify their own code at runtime, making it difficult to analyze statically. These malware samples overwrite their own instructions in memory, decrypting small portions of code just before execution. To capture self-modifying code, analysts use instruction tracing and memory breakpoints in debuggers to detect changes in the executable sections. By observing how the malware decrypts or reconstructs its code, analysts can extract the final payload and save it as a standalone binary for further examination.

Process injection techniques further complicate unpacking efforts by relocating the malicious payload into another process. Some packed malware samples unpack themselves into memory and then inject the extracted payload into a legitimate system process, such as explorer.exe or svchost.exe. This allows the malware to evade detection by running under the guise of a trusted application. Analysts can detect process injection by monitoring API calls like CreateRemoteThread, WriteProcessMemory, or SetThreadContext. Once the injected payload is identified, memory analysis tools can be used to dump the executable from the target process and reconstruct its original form.

Dumping memory is a crucial step in manual unpacking. Once the unpacked payload is located in memory, analysts must extract it and reconstruct a valid executable file. Tools like Process Dump, Volatility, or Scylla allow researchers to capture the memory regions containing the unpacked malware. However, dumped payloads often lack proper PE headers or import tables, which must be reconstructed for the binary to function correctly outside of its original execution context. Tools like Import REConstructor (ImpRec) help rebuild missing import tables, while manual modifications may be required to correct damaged headers or entry points.

Multiple-layer packing is a technique used by sophisticated malware to further complicate unpacking. Some malware samples go through multiple stages of unpacking, where an initial packer extracts an intermediate loader, which then unpacks the final payload. This approach increases the time and effort required to fully analyze the malware. Analysts must iteratively unpack each layer, using debugging and memory dumping techniques at different execution stages until the original payload is recovered. Some malware variants also use nested encryption, requiring decryption keys to be extracted dynamically through breakpoints or API monitoring.

Identifying and bypassing execution delays is another challenge in unpacking malware. Some packed malware samples use sleep obfuscation techniques, where they introduce long delays before executing their unpacked payload. This is intended to outlast sandbox execution time limits or frustrate analysts who are manually stepping through the code. Analysts can bypass execution delays by patching sleep functions, modifying timer values, or accelerating system time artificially. By forcing the malware to execute its unpacking routine without delay, analysts can retrieve the original payload more efficiently.

Understanding and countering packing techniques is an essential skill for malware analysts. Since packed malware attempts to hide its true intent, successfully unpacking it allows security researchers to analyze its functionality, extract IoCs, and develop better detection methods. By using debugging, memory analysis, and API monitoring techniques, analysts can defeat packing methods, retrieve the original malicious payload, and uncover the full scope of the malware's capabilities.

Code Injection and Process Hollowing

Code injection is a sophisticated technique used by malware to execute malicious code within the memory space of legitimate processes. This approach allows attackers to run their payloads while disguising them as trusted system processes, making detection and analysis more difficult. Code injection techniques are widely used by cybercriminals to bypass security defenses, evade antivirus detection, and maintain persistence on infected systems. By injecting malicious code into legitimate applications, malware can operate stealthily, intercept system calls, and manipulate critical functions without directly affecting its original executable.

One of the most common code injection techniques is DLL injection. Dynamic Link Libraries (DLLs) are shared modules loaded by various applications to provide functionality. Malware exploits this mechanism by injecting malicious DLLs into running processes. The attacker uses system API calls like OpenProcess, VirtualAllocEx, WriteProcessMemory, and CreateRemoteThread to allocate memory, write the DLL path, and create a remote thread to execute the injected DLL. Once the DLL is loaded into the target process, the malware can perform various malicious activities, such as keylogging, stealing credentials, or modifying system behavior. Some advanced malware variants use reflective DLL injection, where the malicious DLL is loaded directly into memory without being written to disk, further reducing detection opportunities.

Another technique commonly used by malware is thread hijacking. In this method, the attacker injects malicious code into an existing thread of a legitimate process instead of creating a new thread. This technique is more covert since many security tools monitor the creation of new threads as a sign of suspicious activity. By using functions like SuspendThread, GetThreadContext, WriteProcessMemory, and SetThreadContext, the malware modifies the execution flow of a legitimate thread to point to its malicious payload. Once executed, the injected code runs within the context of the legitimate process, making it harder to detect.

Process injection techniques are not limited to DLL injection and thread hijacking. Another widely used method is APC (Asynchronous

Procedure Call) injection. APCs are designed to execute functions asynchronously in the context of a specific thread. Malware exploits this mechanism by queuing a malicious function in the APC queue of a legitimate process. When the target thread enters an alertable state, it executes the malicious function unknowingly. Attackers use functions such as QueueUserAPC to inject their payloads. Since APC injection relies on an existing process's execution flow, it is more difficult for security tools to detect the injection attempt.

Hooking is another technique that involves modifying system functions to intercept or alter their behavior. Malware can hook API calls at the user-mode level by modifying function pointers in a process's Import Address Table (IAT) or at the kernel level by patching system call tables. Hooking allows malware to manipulate data returned by legitimate functions, redirect execution flows, or spy on user activities. For example, keyloggers often use API hooking to intercept keystrokes captured by functions like GetAsyncKeyState or NtUserGetMessage. By injecting malicious hooks, malware can hide itself from security tools, alter forensic logs, or reroute network traffic for data exfiltration.

Process hollowing is a more advanced form of code injection where malware creates a new process in a suspended state, replaces its memory with malicious code, and then resumes execution. Unlike traditional injection techniques, which insert code into an existing process, process hollowing completely replaces the legitimate executable with a malicious payload. This method is commonly used by sophisticated malware families, including ransomware, trojans, and advanced persistent threats (APTs), to blend in with system processes while executing malicious activities.

The process hollowing technique begins with the malware creating a new process using CreateProcess with the CREATE_SUSPENDED flag. This ensures that the process is loaded into memory but not yet executed. The malware then calls NtUnmapViewOfSection to remove the legitimate code from memory, making space for its malicious payload. Using VirtualAllocEx, the attacker allocates new memory in the target process and writes the malicious payload using WriteProcessMemory. Finally, SetThreadContext is used to modify the entry point of the target process, and ResumeThread is called to start execution, effectively running the malware under the guise of a legitimate application.

Process hollowing is particularly effective at evading detection because security tools often associate a process's name and properties with its expected behavior. If a trusted application like svchost.exe or explorer.exe is running, most security solutions will not flag it as suspicious. However, if that process has been hollowed and replaced with a malicious payload, it can perform unauthorized actions while remaining undetected. This technique is commonly used in ransomware attacks to execute encryption routines silently or in banking trojans to capture financial credentials.

Some malware variants use process doppelgänging, a technique similar to process hollowing but leveraging the Windows Transactional NTFS (TxF) feature. In process doppelgänging, the attacker creates a transaction to modify an executable file, replaces its content with a malicious payload, and then rolls back the transaction to restore the original file. However, the process is already executed using the modified payload. This approach ensures that security tools inspecting the file on disk see the legitimate version, while the system executes the malicious version, making detection even more difficult.

Code injection and process hollowing are widely used in modern cyber threats, making them important areas of focus for security researchers and forensic analysts. Detecting these techniques requires advanced behavioral monitoring, memory forensics, and API call tracing. Tools like Process Explorer and Process Hacker can reveal suspicious process behaviors, such as unusual memory allocations or injected threads. Debugging tools like x64dbg can help analysts trace execution flows and identify code modifications. Additionally, memory forensic tools like Volatility allow researchers to extract and analyze injected payloads from running processes.

Defending against code injection and process hollowing requires a combination of security controls. Endpoint detection and response (EDR) solutions can monitor suspicious memory modifications and API calls associated with these techniques. Behavior-based anomaly detection helps identify unusual process activities, such as legitimate system processes executing unexpected actions. Preventing unauthorized code execution can also be achieved by enforcing process whitelisting, restricting memory execution permissions, and enabling Windows Defender's Attack Surface Reduction (ASR) rules to block process hollowing attempts.

Malware authors continuously refine code injection techniques to improve stealth and evade modern security defenses. As security tools evolve to detect traditional injection methods, attackers adapt by using fileless techniques, memory-only execution, and encrypted payloads. Understanding how code injection and process hollowing work allows security professionals to develop better detection mechanisms and strengthen system defenses against these evasive threats. By analyzing malware that employs these techniques, researchers can gain insights into attacker methodologies and improve overall cybersecurity resilience.

Rootkits and Kernel-Level Malware

Rootkits and kernel-level malware represent some of the most advanced and dangerous cyber threats. These types of malware operate at the deepest layers of an operating system, allowing attackers to gain privileged access, hide malicious activity, and evade detection by traditional security solutions. Unlike user-mode malware, which runs with limited privileges and can often be detected by antivirus software, rootkits and kernel-level malware manipulate the operating system at its core, intercepting system calls, modifying kernel structures, and hiding their presence from security tools. Understanding how these threats work is essential for cybersecurity professionals to detect, analyze, and mitigate them effectively.

A rootkit is a type of malware designed to provide persistent, unauthorized access to a system while concealing its presence. The term "rootkit" originates from the combination of "root," the highest privilege level in Unix-like operating systems, and "kit," referring to a set of tools that enable unauthorized control. Rootkits can exist at different levels within a system, ranging from user-mode rootkits, which modify application-layer processes, to kernel-mode rootkits, which directly manipulate the operating system's core functions. The most sophisticated rootkits operate at the firmware or hypervisor level, making them even more challenging to detect and remove.

Kernel-level rootkits are particularly dangerous because they operate within the kernel, the central part of the operating system responsible for managing hardware, processes, and system security. By running at this privileged level, kernel rootkits can intercept system calls, modify kernel data structures, and manipulate system components without triggering alarms from traditional security software. They can hide files, mask network connections, and even disable security mechanisms such as firewalls and antivirus programs. Since the kernel has direct access to all system resources, a compromised kernel means complete control over the infected machine.

One of the primary techniques used by kernel-level malware is hooking. Hooking involves intercepting function calls or system events to alter their behavior. Malware authors use kernel-mode hooks to hide malicious processes, intercept keyboard input, and redirect file access requests. For example, by hooking functions in the Windows Kernel Patch Protection (PatchGuard), a rootkit can prevent security software from detecting its presence. Hooking can be performed at different levels, including API hooking, inline hooking, and Interrupt Descriptor Table (IDT) hooking, each providing different levels of control over system operations.

Direct Kernel Object Manipulation (DKOM) is another powerful technique used by rootkits to modify kernel data structures without using standard API calls. DKOM allows malware to remove processes from task lists, hide registry entries, and manipulate security tokens to escalate privileges. Since DKOM operates at a low level within the system, traditional security software that relies on API monitoring may fail to detect these modifications. Analysts investigating DKOM-based rootkits must use advanced forensic tools that inspect raw kernel memory rather than relying solely on user-mode detection techniques.

Firmware rootkits represent an even more persistent and stealthy category of malware. Unlike kernel-level rootkits that modify the operating system, firmware rootkits infect the low-level firmware that controls hardware components, such as the BIOS, UEFI, or hardware drivers. Because firmware executes before the operating system loads, a compromised firmware component can persist even after the operating system is reinstalled or the hard drive is replaced. Attackers can use firmware rootkits to modify system boot sequences, inject malicious code into hardware components, and establish long-term persistence on targeted devices. Detecting and removing firmware rootkits often requires specialized hardware-based security measures, such as Trusted Platform Module (TPM) verification and firmware integrity checks.

One of the most well-known examples of kernel-level malware is Stuxnet, a sophisticated cyber weapon designed to sabotage Iran's nuclear program. Stuxnet leveraged multiple zero-day exploits to gain kernel-level access and modify industrial control systems. It used advanced rootkit techniques to hide its presence while manipulating Programmable Logic Controllers (PLCs) to cause physical damage to centrifuges. Stuxnet demonstrated the potential of kernel-level malware to cause real-world harm and highlighted the growing intersection between cybersecurity and national security.

Detection and mitigation of rootkits and kernel-level malware require specialized techniques, as these threats operate beyond the reach of traditional antivirus solutions. Kernel memory analysis tools, such as Volatility and Rekall, allow security researchers to examine raw memory dumps for signs of hidden processes, altered system structures, and suspicious kernel modules. Signature-based detection methods are often ineffective against rootkits, as they modify system components dynamically. Instead, behavioral analysis and integrity checking tools, such as Microsoft's Windows Defender Application Control (WDAC) and Kernel Patch Protection, can help identify unauthorized modifications to the kernel.

Removing rootkits is a complex and often risky process. Since these threats integrate deeply with the operating system, improperly removing a rootkit can cause system instability or render the machine unbootable. In some cases, forensic analysts use bootable security tools, such as Kaspersky Rescue Disk or Trend Micro's RootkitBuster, to scan and remove rootkits before the operating system loads. In extreme cases, where a rootkit has compromised firmware or deeply embedded kernel components, the only reliable method of removal may be a complete system reinstallation or flashing the affected firmware.

As cyber threats evolve, attackers continue to develop more advanced rootkit techniques, including hypervisor-level rootkits, which operate at an even lower level than the kernel. These rootkits modify the hypervisor, the software layer responsible for managing virtual machines, allowing attackers to manipulate all operating systems running on the compromised hardware. Hypervisor rootkits are particularly challenging to detect because they operate below the OS level, making them invisible to traditional security tools. Advanced hardware-based security solutions, such as Intel's Trusted Execution Technology (TXT) and Secure Boot, help mitigate hypervisor-level attacks by ensuring that only trusted code executes at boot time.

The battle between malware authors and security researchers continues as new rootkit techniques emerge. Understanding how rootkits and kernel-level malware operate is essential for developing effective detection and prevention strategies. By leveraging kernel memory analysis, firmware integrity checks, and behavioral anomaly detection, security professionals can enhance their ability to combat these stealthy and persistent threats. While rootkits remain one of the most formidable challenges in cybersecurity, continued research and innovation in security defenses offer hope in the fight against these advanced attacks.

Ransomware Analysis and Decryption Techniques

Ransomware is one of the most damaging types of malware, encrypting files and demanding payment in exchange for decryption. It has evolved into a major cyber threat, targeting individuals, businesses, and even critical infrastructure. Understanding ransomware behavior, analyzing its execution, and identifying potential decryption techniques are crucial for mitigating its impact and developing countermeasures. Security researchers and incident responders use various methods to analyze ransomware, extract valuable indicators of compromise, and, in some cases, recover encrypted files without paying the ransom.

Ransomware typically follows a structured attack pattern, beginning with infection vectors such as phishing emails, malicious downloads, exploit kits, or Remote Desktop Protocol (RDP) brute-force attacks. Once executed, ransomware scans the system for valuable files, encrypts them using cryptographic algorithms, and displays a ransom note demanding payment, usually in cryptocurrency. Some variants delete shadow copies and disable recovery options to prevent victims from restoring their data. Understanding how ransomware spreads and executes helps security professionals develop defenses against future attacks.

Analyzing ransomware starts with setting up a controlled environment to safely execute the malware. Security researchers use isolated virtual machines with restricted network access to prevent the ransomware from communicating with its command-and-control (C2) servers. Dynamic analysis tools, such as Process Monitor and Wireshark, help track system modifications, file encryption behavior, and network activity. By monitoring API calls and registry changes, analysts can identify the ransomware's persistence mechanisms and determine whether it modifies system settings to ensure execution after reboot.

Static analysis provides additional insights into ransomware behavior without executing the malware. Analysts inspect the ransomware binary using tools like PEStudio, IDA Pro, or Ghidra to examine its structure, imported functions, and embedded strings. Many ransomware families use obfuscation techniques to hide their true functionality, encrypting critical strings or packing the executable. By extracting and analyzing these elements, researchers can identify encryption routines, potential hardcoded decryption keys, or weaknesses in the ransomware's implementation.

One of the most critical aspects of ransomware analysis is understanding its encryption mechanism. Ransomware typically uses symmetric encryption (AES) or asymmetric encryption (RSA) to lock files. Some variants generate a unique encryption key for each infected system, storing the decryption key on a remote server controlled by the attackers. More sophisticated ransomware uses hybrid encryption, combining AES for file encryption and RSA to encrypt the AES key, making decryption without the private key extremely difficult. Analyzing the ransomware's encryption logic can reveal whether weak cryptographic implementations or hardcoded keys provide an opportunity for file recovery.

Memory forensics plays a crucial role in identifying decryption keys. Since ransomware needs to access encryption keys during execution, these keys may be temporarily stored in memory. Using tools like Volatility and Process Hacker, analysts can capture memory dumps and search for encryption-related artifacts. If the ransomware does not properly clear memory after encryption, it may be possible to extract the decryption key and recover files without paying the ransom.

Some ransomware families contain coding flaws that allow researchers to develop decryption tools. Poor key management, predictable key generation, or incorrect implementation of cryptographic algorithms can lead to vulnerabilities that security researchers exploit. In the past, ransomware strains like TeslaCrypt, Petya, and Crysis have been successfully decrypted due to weaknesses in their encryption methods. When a decryption tool is available, victims can recover their files without financial loss. Security researchers often share decryption tools on platforms such as No More Ransom, providing free solutions to victims of ransomware attacks.

Network traffic analysis can also provide valuable insights into ransomware behavior. Many ransomware variants communicate with C2 servers to retrieve encryption keys, send infection status updates, or download additional payloads. By analyzing network requests using Wireshark or Fiddler, analysts can identify domain names, IP addresses, or encryption key exchanges. If the ransomware relies on an online key retrieval process, blocking its network communication before encryption is complete may prevent files from being locked. Some ransomware samples use hardcoded C2 domains, which, if taken down, can disrupt their encryption process.

Preventing ransomware attacks requires a multi-layered security approach. Organizations implement endpoint detection and response (EDR) solutions to monitor suspicious file modifications and process executions. Behavior-based detection mechanisms help identify ransomware patterns, such as rapid file encryption, mass file renaming, or attempts to disable system recovery options. Regular backups, stored in offline or immutable storage, provide an essential recovery option in the event of an attack.

Security professionals also use deception techniques to analyze ransomware behavior. Ransomware honeypots, which consist of fake files designed to attract encryption attempts, help researchers study how different variants operate. By monitoring how ransomware interacts with these decoy files, analysts can determine its encryption speed, target file extensions, and evasion techniques. Some ransomware families implement mechanisms to detect sandbox environments and refuse to execute if they suspect they are being analyzed. Researchers counteract these evasion tactics by modifying sandbox configurations or injecting artificial user activity to convince the ransomware that it is running on a real system.

Law enforcement and cybersecurity organizations work together to disrupt ransomware operations by targeting infrastructure used by ransomware gangs. Takedown efforts focus on dismantling C2 networks, seizing cryptocurrency wallets, and arresting individuals behind major ransomware campaigns. Ransomware-as-a-Service (RaaS) models, where cybercriminals lease ransomware kits to affiliates, have contributed to the rapid spread of ransomware attacks. By disrupting these services, authorities aim to reduce the overall impact of ransomware on global organizations.

Understanding ransomware analysis and decryption techniques is essential for security researchers, incident responders, and victims seeking to recover encrypted data. As ransomware continues to evolve with more advanced encryption schemes, the ability to analyze, detect, and counter these threats remains a top priority in cybersecurity. Researchers continually develop new tools and methodologies to identify weaknesses in ransomware operations, helping to mitigate its devastating impact on businesses and individuals.

Banking Trojans and Credential Stealers

Banking Trojans and credential stealers are among the most financially motivated types of malware, designed to compromise online banking accounts, payment systems, and personal credentials. These threats target individuals, businesses, and financial institutions by intercepting sensitive information, such as login credentials, credit card details, and authentication tokens. Cybercriminals use these stolen credentials to conduct fraudulent transactions, sell account access on the dark web, or facilitate large-scale financial fraud. As online banking and digital transactions continue to grow, banking Trojans and credential stealers remain a persistent and evolving threat.

Banking Trojans are a specialized type of malware designed to infiltrate banking systems and steal financial information. They typically operate by injecting malicious code into legitimate banking websites, tricking users into entering their credentials on fake login pages, or capturing keystrokes during authentication. Many banking Trojans use advanced evasion techniques to bypass security mechanisms such as two-factor authentication (2FA) and biometric verification. Some variants are capable of modifying transaction details in real time, allowing attackers to redirect funds to their own accounts without the victim noticing the changes.

One of the most well-known banking Trojans is Zeus, which emerged in the late 2000s and became the foundation for many subsequent variants. Zeus infected millions of devices worldwide, using web injections and keylogging to steal online banking credentials. Variants like Gameover Zeus expanded its capabilities by adding peer-to-peer (P2P) networking for decentralized command-and-control (C2) communication, making it more resilient to takedown efforts. Other notable banking Trojans, such as Dridex, TrickBot, and QakBot, have followed similar paths, continuously evolving to evade detection and incorporate new attack techniques.

Credential stealers, while similar to banking Trojans, have a broader focus and are designed to harvest login credentials from various sources, including web browsers, email clients, and password managers. These malware strains operate by extracting saved passwords, capturing keystrokes, or stealing authentication cookies that allow attackers to bypass login requirements. Credential stealers are often distributed through phishing campaigns, malicious attachments, or compromised websites that deliver drive-by downloads. Once installed, they silently collect credentials and send them to an attacker-controlled server, where they can be used for further attacks or sold on underground marketplaces.

Many credential stealers target web browsers, as they store vast amounts of login data for user convenience. Malware such as RedLine Stealer and Raccoon Stealer specialize in extracting saved passwords, browser cookies, and autofill data from popular browsers like Chrome, Firefox, and Edge. By stealing session cookies, attackers can hijack active accounts without needing the victim's password, effectively bypassing security measures like multi-factor authentication (MFA). Some credential stealers also extract data from cryptocurrency wallets, enabling cybercriminals to drain digital assets from compromised accounts.

Banking Trojans and credential stealers often use multiple infection vectors to reach their targets. Phishing emails remain one of the most effective distribution methods, using deceptive messages that trick users into downloading malicious attachments or clicking on fraudulent links. Cybercriminals craft emails that appear to be from legitimate banks, payment processors, or government agencies, urging recipients to verify their accounts or reset their passwords. Once the victim interacts with the malicious content, the malware is executed, embedding itself within the system and beginning data exfiltration.

Exploit kits are another method used to distribute banking Trojans and credential stealers. These automated attack frameworks take advantage of software vulnerabilities to install malware without user interaction. When a victim visits a compromised website, the exploit kit scans their system for outdated software, such as unpatched web browsers or plugins. If a vulnerability is found, the exploit kit delivers the malware payload silently in the background. Well-known exploit kits such as Rig and Fallout have been used to distribute banking Trojans like Dridex and TrickBot, enabling widespread infections across unprotected systems.

Many banking Trojans incorporate remote access capabilities, allowing attackers to control infected devices and manipulate online transactions. Remote Access Trojans (RATs) enable cybercriminals to interact with banking websites in real time, injecting fraudulent payment details while victims unknowingly approve transactions. Some banking Trojans use "web fakes" or "man-in-the-browser" (MitB) techniques, altering the display of a banking website on the victim's screen. This deception allows attackers to trick users into approving unauthorized transfers while displaying seemingly normal account balances and transaction histories.

Detection and mitigation of banking Trojans and credential stealers require a combination of security tools and best practices. Endpoint detection and response (EDR) solutions help identify suspicious activities, such as unauthorized process injections, keystroke logging, and abnormal network traffic. Web filtering and secure email gateways reduce the risk of phishing attacks, preventing malicious emails from reaching potential victims. Multi-factor authentication adds an extra layer of security, making it more difficult for attackers to access accounts even if credentials are stolen.

Behavioral analysis plays a crucial role in detecting banking Trojans and credential stealers, as many variants use polymorphic techniques to evade signature-based detection. Security researchers use sandbox environments to execute malware samples and observe their interactions with banking websites. By analyzing API calls, file modifications, and network communications, analysts can identify patterns that indicate credential theft or financial fraud attempts. Advanced machine learning algorithms help detect previously unknown variants by recognizing suspicious behaviors and anomalies in user activity.

Law enforcement agencies and cybersecurity organizations collaborate to dismantle large-scale banking Trojan operations. Takedown efforts involve disrupting command-and-control servers, seizing attacker infrastructure, and arresting individuals involved in cybercrime networks. Operations targeting botnets controlled by banking Trojans, such as the takedown of the TrickBot network, have demonstrated the effectiveness of coordinated efforts in reducing the impact of financial malware. However, cybercriminals continually adapt, developing new variants and techniques to bypass security measures.

The rise of mobile banking has led to an increase in mobile banking Trojans, which specifically target smartphones and tablets. These malware strains masquerade as legitimate banking apps or use overlay attacks to intercept user credentials during login attempts. Mobile banking Trojans like Anubis, Cerberus, and Alien infect Android devices, often distributed through fake app stores or malicious APK files. These threats exploit accessibility services and permission abuse to gain full control over the device, capturing keystrokes, intercepting SMS-based authentication codes, and even taking screenshots of banking transactions.

Preventing infections from banking Trojans and credential stealers requires user awareness, secure browsing habits, and robust cybersecurity defenses. Individuals should avoid downloading apps from untrusted sources, regularly update their software, and use password managers to generate and store unique credentials. Organizations should enforce strict security policies, conduct phishing awareness training, and implement advanced threat detection solutions to protect against evolving financial malware threats. As cybercriminals continue to refine their techniques, proactive security measures and ongoing research remain essential in the fight against banking Trojans and credential stealers.

Fileless Malware and Memory-Resident Threats

Fileless malware and memory-resident threats represent a sophisticated evolution in cyber threats, designed to evade traditional security solutions by operating entirely in memory. Unlike conventional malware, which relies on executable files stored on disk, fileless malware does not leave traces in the file system, making detection and forensic analysis significantly more challenging. These threats take advantage of legitimate system processes and built-in administrative tools to execute malicious payloads without writing files to disk. By leveraging trusted applications such as PowerShell, Windows Management Instrumentation (WMI), and scripting languages, attackers can achieve persistence, execute commands, and exfiltrate data while remaining largely undetected.

One of the primary techniques used in fileless attacks is PowerShell exploitation. PowerShell is a powerful scripting language built into Windows that allows administrators to automate system tasks. Attackers abuse PowerShell to download, execute, and inject malicious code directly into memory. Since PowerShell is a legitimate and widely used tool, security software often does not flag its execution as suspicious. Malicious PowerShell scripts can be embedded in phishing emails, executed through malicious macros in Office documents, or delivered via web-based attacks. By using obfuscated commands and encoded payloads, attackers further complicate detection and analysis.

Windows Management Instrumentation (WMI) is another commonly abused technology in fileless attacks. WMI is a powerful framework that allows administrators to manage and monitor Windows systems remotely. Attackers leverage WMI to execute scripts, create persistent backdoors, and maintain control over infected machines without dropping files onto the disk. WMI-based attacks can be used for reconnaissance, data exfiltration, and lateral movement within a network. Since WMI is an integral part of the Windows operating system, blocking or restricting its functionality without affecting legitimate operations is challenging.

Another form of fileless malware execution involves the abuse of Microsoft Office macros. Malicious documents containing embedded Visual Basic for Applications (VBA) scripts are commonly used in phishing campaigns. When an unsuspecting user opens the document and enables macros, the embedded script executes malicious PowerShell or WMI commands, launching a fileless attack. These macros often download additional payloads, escalate privileges, or establish persistent access through registry modifications. Since Office macros are a legitimate feature, attackers use social engineering tactics to convince users to enable them, bypassing built-in security controls.

Code injection techniques play a crucial role in fileless malware operations, allowing attackers to execute malicious code within the memory space of legitimate processes. Process hollowing, reflective DLL injection, and APC (Asynchronous Procedure Call) injection are commonly used techniques. Process hollowing involves creating a new legitimate process in a suspended state, replacing its memory with malicious code, and then resuming execution. Reflective DLL injection allows malware to load a DLL directly into memory without writing it to disk, making it invisible to traditional antivirus scanners. APC injection manipulates threads within a legitimate process to execute malicious functions, further obfuscating the attack.

Credential theft and privilege escalation are frequently observed in fileless malware campaigns. Attackers use tools such as Mimikatz to extract credentials from memory, enabling them to escalate privileges, move laterally across networks, and gain access to high-value systems. Since Mimikatz operates entirely in memory, it leaves no files behind, making forensic investigations more difficult. Fileless malware often exploits known vulnerabilities to inject itself into privileged processes, ensuring continued access and persistence without leaving traditional forensic evidence.

Lateral movement is another key objective of fileless malware attacks. Once initial access is gained, attackers use built-in Windows tools such as PsExec and Remote Desktop Protocol (RDP) to move laterally across the network. Since these tools are legitimate administrative utilities, security solutions may not flag their use as malicious. By executing commands remotely and injecting code into legitimate system processes, attackers can compromise multiple endpoints without deploying additional files, reducing their chances of detection.

Persistence mechanisms in fileless malware rely on registry modifications, scheduled tasks, and WMI event subscriptions. Instead of writing executables to disk, attackers store malicious scripts or payloads directly in registry keys. These scripts execute each time the system starts or when a specific trigger event occurs. Scheduled tasks can be created to execute PowerShell scripts at predefined intervals, ensuring continued control over an infected system. WMI event subscriptions allow attackers to execute scripts based on system events, such as user logins or process creation, providing a stealthy method of persistence.

Network-based detection is one of the few reliable ways to identify fileless malware activity. Since these threats operate entirely in memory, traditional antivirus solutions relying on signature-based detection often fail to identify them. Security analysts use network monitoring tools to detect suspicious PowerShell execution, abnormal WMI activity, and unauthorized administrative commands. Indicators such as unusual network traffic, unexpected process interactions, and encoded PowerShell commands can help identify fileless attacks in progress.

Memory forensics is another essential technique for detecting and analyzing fileless malware. Since no files are stored on disk, forensic analysts must extract and examine live memory to identify malicious artifacts. Tools such as Volatility and Rekall allow researchers to analyze memory dumps, search for injected code, and extract process-related information. By identifying unauthorized modifications to system processes, analysts can reconstruct the attack chain and determine how the malware achieved execution and persistence.

Threat hunting strategies for fileless malware focus on behavioral analysis and anomaly detection. Security teams implement heuristic-based detection techniques to monitor script execution, identify unusual process activity, and flag unauthorized use of administrative tools. Machine learning models analyze system behavior to detect deviations from normal activity, helping to identify fileless malware tactics before they cause significant damage. Continuous monitoring and proactive defense measures are essential in combating these advanced threats.

Mitigating fileless malware requires a multi-layered security approach. Organizations should enforce the principle of least privilege, restricting administrative access and limiting the execution of scripting tools such as PowerShell and WMI. Application whitelisting prevents unauthorized scripts from executing, reducing the risk of fileless attacks. Endpoint Detection and Response (EDR) solutions provide real-time monitoring of memory activity, helping detect and respond to fileless threats. Regular security training for employees helps reduce the success rate of phishing attacks, a common delivery method for fileless malware.

As cyber threats continue to evolve, fileless malware and memory-resident attacks pose a growing challenge to traditional security defenses. By leveraging legitimate system processes and operating entirely in memory, these threats evade conventional detection mechanisms, requiring security professionals to adopt advanced forensic techniques, behavioral monitoring, and proactive threat-hunting strategies. Understanding how fileless malware operates and the techniques used by attackers enables organizations to strengthen their defenses and minimize the impact of these stealthy cyber threats.

Keyloggers and Screen Scrapers

Keyloggers and screen scrapers are stealthy forms of malware designed to capture user input and on-screen activity, often with the intent of stealing sensitive information. Cybercriminals use these techniques to obtain credentials, financial data, personal communications, and other confidential information without the victim's knowledge. Because they operate in the background and do not always trigger security alerts, they remain a persistent threat to individuals and organizations. Understanding how keyloggers and screen scrapers work is crucial for detecting, mitigating, and preventing these attacks.

Keyloggers function by recording keystrokes as they are entered on a keyboard. They capture every letter, number, and special character typed by a user, including login credentials, credit card details, messages, and search queries. Once the keystrokes are recorded, the data is stored locally or transmitted to an attacker's remote server. Keyloggers can be categorized into software-based and hardware-based variants, each with different methods of operation and levels of stealth.

Software keyloggers are the most common type and are often installed on a system through malicious downloads, phishing emails, or exploit kits. They operate at different levels within the operating system, including user-mode, kernel-mode, and firmware-level implementations. User-mode keyloggers rely on API hooking techniques to intercept keystrokes as they pass through the operating system's input handling functions. They commonly use Windows API functions such as GetAsyncKeyState, GetKeyState, or SetWindowsHookEx to monitor keyboard input without requiring elevated privileges. Because these functions are intended for legitimate applications, malware developers exploit them to capture keystrokes stealthily.

Kernel-mode keyloggers operate at a lower level within the operating system, intercepting keystrokes before they reach applications. By modifying the keyboard driver or injecting malicious code into the kernel, they can capture keystrokes directly from hardware-level input buffers. Kernel-mode keyloggers are harder to detect than user-mode versions because they do not rely on system API functions that security software typically monitors. However, implementing a kernel-mode keylogger requires advanced knowledge of operating system internals and may trigger security mechanisms such as Windows Kernel Patch Protection (PatchGuard).

Firmware-based keyloggers take stealth one step further by infecting a computer's BIOS, UEFI firmware, or hardware peripherals such as keyboards and USB devices. These keyloggers operate independently of the operating system, making them extremely difficult to detect and remove. Since they reside in hardware, they persist even after an operating system is reinstalled or a hard drive is replaced. Attackers use firmware-level keyloggers in highly targeted attacks, often against high-value individuals or organizations.

Screen scrapers, also known as screen loggers, operate by capturing visual data displayed on a user's monitor. Unlike keyloggers, which only record typed input, screen scrapers take screenshots or extract pixel data to reconstruct what the user sees. These attacks are particularly useful for capturing information that keyloggers cannot, such as virtual keyboards, CAPTCHA responses, or credentials entered via clipboard copy-paste functions. Screen scrapers can be embedded in malware payloads, remote access trojans (RATs), or malicious browser extensions.

One method used by screen scrapers is direct screen capture through API calls. Malware can use Windows API functions such as BitBlt, PrintWindow, or GetDC to capture the contents of the active window or the entire screen. These screenshots are then saved locally or sent to an attacker's server. Some advanced screen scrapers analyze the captured images using optical character recognition (OCR) to extract text from screenshots, allowing attackers to obtain credentials even if they are not typed manually.

Another technique employed by screen scrapers is video recording. Some malware variants continuously record the user's screen activity, capturing everything they do in real time. This method is particularly effective in espionage and surveillance campaigns, where attackers need to monitor a victim's actions over an extended period. Captured video files are usually compressed and exfiltrated in segments to avoid detection.

Screen scrapers are often used in conjunction with keyloggers to maximize data theft. By combining keystroke logging with screen capture, attackers can obtain full login credentials, including those entered using on-screen keyboards or password managers. This approach is commonly used in banking malware, where attackers attempt to bypass security mechanisms designed to prevent keylogging attacks. Some banking trojans, such as Zeus and SpyEye, integrate both keylogging and screen scraping capabilities to target financial transactions.

Detecting keyloggers and screen scrapers requires a combination of security tools and behavioral analysis. Traditional antivirus software relies on signature-based detection to identify known keylogger variants, but this approach is ineffective against new or customized malware. Behavior-based detection, which monitors unusual system activity such as unauthorized API calls, suspicious file modifications, or abnormal network traffic, is more effective at identifying stealthy keyloggers and screen scrapers.

Memory forensics plays an important role in detecting these threats. Since many keyloggers and screen scrapers operate entirely in memory without leaving disk traces, forensic analysts use tools like Volatility to examine active processes, detect injected code, and identify hidden malware components. Analysts look for anomalies such as unexpected hooks in keyboard input functions, unauthorized access to the screen buffer, or unusual connections to remote servers.

Mitigation strategies for keyloggers and screen scrapers include implementing multi-factor authentication (MFA) to reduce the impact of stolen credentials. Even if an attacker captures a password, they would still need an additional authentication factor, such as a one-time code or biometric verification, to gain access. Using virtual keyboards, password managers with automatic form filling, and anti-keylogging tools can also help protect against keylogging threats.

Organizations can strengthen defenses by enforcing strict security policies, regularly updating software, and monitoring privileged access to input devices and screen capture functions. Endpoint Detection and Response (EDR) solutions provide real-time monitoring of system behavior, helping to identify and block malicious keylogging and screen scraping activities. Network segmentation, intrusion detection systems (IDS), and access control measures further reduce the risk of credential theft.

Cybercriminals continue to refine keylogging and screen scraping techniques, incorporating more advanced evasion tactics to bypass modern security measures. Some malware variants use encryption to hide keystroke logs, employ process hollowing to inject themselves into legitimate applications, or leverage fileless execution techniques to operate entirely in memory. As these threats evolve, security professionals must continuously adapt their detection and prevention strategies to stay ahead of attackers. Understanding the methods used by keyloggers and screen scrapers enables organizations to implement effective countermeasures and protect sensitive information from unauthorized access.

Botnets and Distributed Malware

Botnets and distributed malware represent some of the most powerful and persistent threats in cybersecurity. A botnet is a network of compromised computers, known as bots or zombies, controlled by an attacker, often referred to as the botmaster or bot herder. These infected devices operate under remote instructions, executing malicious activities such as distributed denial-of-service (DDoS) attacks, spam distribution, credential theft, and financial fraud. Botnets leverage the scale of distributed systems, allowing cybercriminals to coordinate attacks, evade detection, and maximize their impact.

The infection process of a botnet begins with malware deployment. Cybercriminals use various infection vectors, including phishing emails, malicious downloads, exploit kits, and brute-force attacks, to compromise devices. Once a device is infected, the malware establishes communication with the botnet's command-and-control (C2) server. This C2 infrastructure acts as the central hub for managing the botnet, issuing commands, distributing updates, and retrieving stolen data. Some botnets operate using centralized C2 models, where all infected machines communicate with a single server, while others adopt decentralized architectures to increase resilience against takedown efforts.

One of the most well-known botnet structures is the centralized model, which relies on a single or a small number of C2 servers to control infected machines. While this approach provides efficient management, it also introduces a single point of failure. If security researchers or law enforcement agencies identify and dismantle the C2 server, the entire botnet can be disrupted. To counteract this vulnerability, cybercriminals have developed decentralized botnet architectures, such as peer-to-peer (P2P) botnets, where infected machines communicate directly with each other instead of relying on a central server. This makes detection and disruption significantly more challenging.

Botnets serve multiple purposes, depending on the intent of the attacker. One of the most common uses of botnets is launching DDoS attacks, where thousands or millions of infected devices flood a target system with traffic, overwhelming its resources and rendering it inaccessible. DDoS botnets, such as Mirai, have demonstrated the devastating potential of these attacks, taking down major websites, financial institutions, and even internet infrastructure providers. Mirai specifically targeted Internet of Things (IoT) devices, exploiting weak default credentials to build a massive botnet capable of generating unprecedented levels of traffic.

Another widespread use of botnets is in financial fraud and credential theft. Banking Trojans, such as Zeus and Dridex, operate as botnets by infecting devices, capturing login credentials, and transmitting stolen data to attackers. These botnets continuously evolve, incorporating advanced evasion techniques such as process injection, encrypted communication channels, and polymorphic code to avoid detection. Cybercriminals use stolen credentials for unauthorized transactions, account takeovers, and money laundering schemes, often selling access to compromised accounts on underground forums.

Botnets also play a significant role in the distribution of spam and phishing campaigns. Many botnets are configured to send massive volumes of spam emails containing malicious attachments or phishing links. These emails often impersonate legitimate organizations, tricking recipients into opening infected documents or entering credentials on fraudulent websites. Spam botnets, such as Cutwail and Kelihos, have been responsible for large-scale email fraud operations, distributing ransomware, spyware, and other malware to unsuspecting victims. The ability to distribute malware globally through botnets increases the scale and effectiveness of cybercriminal operations.

Cryptojacking is another major activity facilitated by botnets. In this scenario, infected devices are used to mine cryptocurrency for the attacker, consuming system resources and electricity without the owner's knowledge. Cryptojacking botnets, such as Smominru and WannaMine, exploit vulnerabilities in unpatched systems, deploying mining software that runs in the background. While cryptojacking does not cause immediate data loss, it significantly degrades system performance, increases energy costs, and shortens hardware lifespan. As cryptocurrency mining becomes more profitable, cybercriminals continue to develop and deploy cryptojacking malware through botnets.

Advanced botnets incorporate sophisticated evasion techniques to avoid detection and removal. Many botnets use fast-flux domain switching, where C2 server addresses change frequently to prevent tracking. Domain Generation Algorithms (DGA) create new domain names dynamically, making it difficult for security teams to block botnet communications. Some botnets implement encrypted communication channels using HTTPS, TOR, or custom encryption protocols, ensuring that traffic between infected devices and C2 servers remains undetected by traditional network monitoring tools.

Detection and mitigation of botnets require a multi-layered security approach. Network traffic analysis plays a crucial role in identifying botnet activity. Security teams monitor for unusual outbound connections, abnormal DNS requests, and communication patterns associated with known botnets. Intrusion detection systems (IDS) and intrusion prevention systems (IPS) help block botnet-related traffic, preventing compromised devices from communicating with C2 servers. Implementing endpoint detection and response (EDR) solutions allows organizations to detect and remediate infections at the device level.

Law enforcement agencies and cybersecurity organizations collaborate to dismantle major botnet operations. Takedown efforts focus on identifying and shutting down C2 servers, seizing attacker infrastructure, and prosecuting those responsible. Notable botnet takedowns include the dismantling of the Kelihos botnet, the disruption of Gameover Zeus, and the seizure of TrickBot servers. However, botnet operators quickly adapt by deploying new variants, migrating to different hosting providers, or implementing decentralized communication methods.

Preventing botnet infections requires proactive cybersecurity measures. Organizations and individuals should apply security patches regularly to eliminate known vulnerabilities exploited by botnets. Using strong, unique passwords for all devices, particularly IoT systems, reduces the risk of compromise. Disabling unnecessary remote access protocols, such as Remote Desktop Protocol (RDP) and Telnet, helps prevent brute-force attacks that botnets use to gain access to systems. Implementing network segmentation limits the spread of infections, preventing botnets from gaining control over critical systems.

Botnets and distributed malware continue to evolve, leveraging new attack vectors and advanced evasion techniques. Their ability to operate on a massive scale makes them a persistent threat in cybersecurity. Understanding how botnets function, identifying their communication methods, and deploying effective countermeasures are essential steps in defending against these widespread and evolving cyber threats. Security professionals must stay ahead of attackers by continuously monitoring emerging botnet trends and improving detection and response capabilities.

Malware in IoT and Embedded Systems

The rise of the Internet of Things (IoT) and embedded systems has introduced new attack surfaces for cybercriminals. IoT devices, including smart home appliances, industrial control systems, medical devices, and automotive systems, often lack robust security mechanisms, making them attractive targets for malware. Unlike traditional computers, many IoT and embedded devices operate with limited processing power, proprietary firmware, and outdated security protocols, making malware detection and mitigation challenging. Attackers exploit these weaknesses to deploy malware that can compromise privacy, disrupt operations, or even cause physical harm in critical infrastructure environments.

IoT malware is designed to exploit vulnerabilities in connected devices, often using weak or default credentials, unpatched software, or misconfigured settings to gain access. Many IoT devices ship with factory-set usernames and passwords that users fail to change, allowing attackers to perform large-scale brute-force attacks to compromise them. Once infected, an IoT device can be used as part of a botnet, enabling distributed denial-of-service (DDoS) attacks, cryptocurrency mining, or further propagation of malware to other networked systems.

One of the most infamous examples of IoT malware is Mirai, which emerged in 2016 and rapidly infected millions of internet-connected devices. Mirai targeted IP cameras, routers, and other IoT devices by scanning for those using default credentials and gaining control over them. Once compromised, these devices were recruited into a massive botnet used to launch record-breaking DDoS attacks against major websites, internet infrastructure, and service providers. The success of Mirai led to the development of multiple variants, each with enhanced evasion techniques and improved infection methods.

IoT malware often leverages weak authentication mechanisms to establish persistence on devices. Many embedded systems lack the capability for robust authentication, relying instead on hardcoded passwords or insecure communication protocols. Attackers exploit these weaknesses to install rootkits or firmware-level malware that can survive reboots and firmware updates. In some cases, malware modifies device firmware to embed a backdoor, allowing persistent remote access even if the device is reset to factory settings.

Another significant challenge in securing IoT devices is the lack of regular software updates. Many manufacturers fail to provide security patches, leaving devices vulnerable to known exploits. Attackers scan the internet for outdated devices running vulnerable firmware, deploying automated scripts to compromise them. Some malware variants exploit universal plug-and-play (UPnP) vulnerabilities to bypass firewalls and gain direct access to IoT devices behind network routers. Once inside a network, malware can pivot to other connected devices, including traditional computers and critical infrastructure systems.

Industrial IoT (IIoT) and embedded systems used in manufacturing, energy, healthcare, and transportation sectors are particularly vulnerable to malware attacks. Many of these devices operate in mission-critical environments where downtime can have severe consequences. Malware targeting IIoT systems can disrupt production lines, manipulate sensor readings, or cause physical damage to machinery. The 2010 Stuxnet worm demonstrated the potential for malware to target industrial control systems (ICS). Stuxnet was designed to sabotage Iran's nuclear enrichment program by infecting programmable logic controllers (PLCs), demonstrating how malware can have real-world, physical effects.

IoT malware also poses a significant risk to healthcare devices, including pacemakers, insulin pumps, and diagnostic machines. Many of these devices connect to hospital networks for remote monitoring and updates, making them potential entry points for cyberattacks. Malware that compromises medical devices can manipulate dosage levels, alter patient data, or render devices inoperable, posing a direct threat to patient safety. The lack of standardized security measures across healthcare IoT devices increases the risk of malware infections and unauthorized access.

Another growing trend is the use of IoT malware for cryptocurrency mining, also known as cryptojacking. Attackers deploy mining malware on IoT devices with sufficient processing power, such as smart TVs, routers, and surveillance cameras. While IoT devices are not as powerful as traditional computers, the sheer number of infected devices can generate significant profits for attackers. Cryptojacking malware runs in the background, consuming system resources and shortening device lifespan. Many users remain unaware of these infections, as IoT malware often lacks visible symptoms beyond sluggish performance.

Mobile and automotive IoT systems are also increasingly targeted by malware. Modern vehicles integrate numerous IoT components, including GPS navigation, remote access systems, and onboard diagnostics. Malware targeting automotive IoT can manipulate vehicle controls, disable safety features, or track user movements. Security researchers have demonstrated proof-of-concept attacks where malware remotely disables brakes or unlocks car doors, highlighting the potential dangers of unsecured IoT in vehicles.

Mitigating IoT malware requires a combination of security best practices, firmware updates, and network monitoring. Device manufacturers must implement stronger authentication mechanisms, such as multi-factor authentication (MFA) and certificate-based authentication, to prevent unauthorized access. Users should change default credentials, disable unnecessary network services, and regularly update firmware to patch vulnerabilities.

Network segmentation plays a crucial role in limiting the spread of IoT malware. Organizations should isolate IoT devices from critical systems using VLANs, firewalls, and intrusion detection systems (IDS). By restricting communication between IoT devices and sensitive infrastructure, the impact of malware infections can be minimized. Security teams should also monitor network traffic for unusual patterns, such as unexpected outbound connections or high-bandwidth usage, which could indicate IoT malware activity.

Threat intelligence and behavior-based detection are essential for identifying new IoT malware variants. Traditional signature-based detection methods often fail against rapidly evolving malware strains. Machine learning and AI-powered security solutions help detect anomalies in device behavior, flagging potential infections based on deviations from normal activity. Some security solutions use honeypots—intentionally vulnerable devices deployed to attract and analyze malware—to gather intelligence on new threats and develop mitigation strategies.

Regulatory efforts are also underway to improve IoT security. Governments and cybersecurity organizations are pushing for security standards that require manufacturers to implement stronger protections in IoT devices. Regulations such as the IoT Cybersecurity Improvement Act in the United States mandate secure development practices, vulnerability reporting, and authentication requirements for IoT devices used in government systems. However, widespread adoption of secure IoT standards remains a challenge, as many manufacturers prioritize cost and ease of use over security.

The expansion of IoT in homes, businesses, and critical infrastructure makes it an increasingly attractive target for cybercriminals. As malware continues to evolve, security professionals must remain vigilant in monitoring new attack vectors and implementing effective defenses. Strengthening IoT security at the device, network, and regulatory levels is essential for mitigating the risks posed by malware in IoT and embedded systems.

Mobile Malware: Android and iOS Threats

Mobile malware has become an increasing threat as smartphones and tablets have become essential in daily life. With millions of people using mobile devices for banking, communication, social media, and work, cybercriminals see them as valuable targets for financial fraud, espionage, and data theft. Android and iOS, the two dominant mobile operating systems, face different types of threats due to their distinct architectures and security models. While Android's open nature makes it more susceptible to malware distribution, iOS is not immune to sophisticated attacks, especially through targeted exploits and jailbreaking techniques.

Android devices are the primary target for mobile malware due to the flexibility of the operating system and the availability of third-party app stores. Malicious apps often masquerade as legitimate applications, tricking users into downloading them. Once installed, these apps can steal credentials, track user activity, send premium-rate SMS messages, or install additional malware. Some threats gain administrative privileges using root exploits, allowing them to persist even after a factory reset. Attackers use various techniques to distribute Android malware, including phishing links, fake software updates, and trojanized versions of popular apps.

One of the most common Android malware types is banking trojans. These trojans target financial applications, intercepting login credentials and authentication codes. Some variants use overlay attacks, where a fake login screen is displayed over a legitimate banking app, tricking users into entering their credentials. Others abuse Android's accessibility services to read text messages, capture keystrokes, or manipulate user interactions. Notable banking trojans like Anubis, Cerberus, and BRATA continuously evolve to bypass security mechanisms and steal sensitive financial data.

Adware is another widespread form of Android malware. Malicious adware generates revenue for cybercriminals by displaying intrusive advertisements, redirecting users to fraudulent websites, or installing additional apps without consent. Some adware strains use advanced persistence techniques, such as modifying system settings or embedding themselves in device firmware, making them difficult to remove. Infected devices experience battery drain, decreased performance, and excessive data usage due to constant ad requests.

Ransomware has also emerged as a growing threat in the mobile ecosystem. Mobile ransomware locks the device screen or encrypts files, demanding payment for restoration. Some variants use scare tactics, displaying fake law enforcement messages accusing users of illegal activities. Others exploit accessibility services to change device settings and prevent users from removing the malware. While mobile ransomware is less common than its desktop counterpart, its impact on victims can be severe, especially when targeting business devices containing critical data.

Spyware and stalkerware are particularly concerning forms of mobile malware. These threats are used for surveillance, capturing messages, call logs, GPS locations, and even microphone recordings without the user's knowledge. Some spyware variants are deployed by cybercriminals for espionage, while others are used by individuals for stalking or domestic abuse. Commercial spyware like Pegasus has demonstrated how mobile devices can be infiltrated using zero-click exploits, allowing attackers to gain complete control over a target's phone without requiring user interaction.

Malware distribution on Android often involves deceptive app permissions. Many malicious apps request excessive permissions, such as access to SMS messages, contacts, and system settings, which they use for malicious activities. Google Play Protect, the built-in Android security feature, scans apps for potential threats, but attackers continuously find ways to bypass detection. Some malware samples employ time-based execution delays or encryption techniques to avoid being flagged by security scanners.

iOS, while generally more secure due to Apple's walled-garden approach, is not completely immune to malware. The App Store's strict security policies make it difficult for malicious apps to reach users, but sophisticated attackers exploit vulnerabilities to compromise iOS devices. Jailbreaking, which allows users to bypass Apple's restrictions and install unauthorized apps, increases the risk of malware infections. Jailbroken devices lose many of Apple's built-in security protections, making them vulnerable to spyware, keyloggers, and malicious tweaks.

iOS malware is often delivered through zero-day exploits and social engineering tactics. Attackers use malicious websites, phishing emails, or compromised app certificates to install unauthorized applications. Enterprise provisioning profiles, originally designed for corporate app distribution, have been abused to sideload malware onto non-jailbroken devices. By tricking users into installing a rogue configuration profile, attackers gain the ability to install apps outside the App Store, bypassing Apple's security checks.

Advanced persistent threats (APTs) targeting iOS devices are usually linked to nation-state actors. Spyware like Pegasus has been used to infiltrate high-profile targets, exploiting zero-click vulnerabilities in iMessage, FaceTime, and Safari. These sophisticated threats can extract data from encrypted messaging apps, track real-time locations, and remotely activate cameras or microphones. Since iOS malware operates stealthily, detecting infections often requires forensic analysis using specialized security tools.

Mobile malware detection and mitigation require a combination of security best practices and technical countermeasures. Users should avoid downloading apps from unofficial sources, review app permissions carefully, and keep their devices updated with the latest security patches. Security researchers analyze mobile malware using dynamic analysis tools like Frida, MobSF, and JADX to decompile apps, inspect network traffic, and identify malicious behaviors.

Organizations implement mobile device management (MDM) solutions to enforce security policies, restrict app installations, and monitor device activity. Endpoint protection solutions for mobile devices detect malware signatures, behavioral anomalies, and unauthorized system modifications. Network-level defenses, such as DNS filtering and VPN security, help prevent malware from communicating with command-and-control servers.

Cybercriminals continue to refine mobile malware techniques, leveraging social engineering, exploit chains, and advanced evasion tactics to compromise devices. As mobile usage grows, attackers increasingly target both Android and iOS ecosystems, exploiting vulnerabilities and user habits to distribute malware. Strengthening mobile security awareness, enforcing security controls, and staying informed about emerging threats are essential to protecting devices from malicious attacks.

MacOS and Linux Malware Analysis

MacOS and Linux have traditionally been considered more secure than Windows, but they are not immune to malware threats. While these operating systems benefit from stronger security architectures and lower market share, attackers increasingly target them as their adoption grows in enterprise and personal environments. MacOS and Linux malware have become more sophisticated, leveraging privilege escalation, rootkits, and supply chain attacks to compromise systems. Understanding the techniques used to analyze malware on these platforms is essential for cybersecurity professionals to detect, mitigate, and prevent infections effectively.

MacOS malware often relies on social engineering and application-based exploits to infiltrate systems. Since macOS includes security features such as Gatekeeper, System Integrity Protection (SIP), and XProtect, attackers must find ways to bypass these protections. Many macOS malware variants are distributed via trojanized applications, malicious browser extensions, or compromised software updates. Common attack vectors include fake Adobe Flash Player installers, pirated software, and phishing campaigns that trick users into granting administrative privileges to malicious applications. Once executed, macOS malware can modify system settings, install persistent backdoors, and exfiltrate sensitive data.

Linux malware, on the other hand, often targets servers, cloud infrastructure, and IoT devices rather than desktop users. Linux-based systems are widely used in enterprise environments, making them attractive targets for cybercriminals and state-sponsored actors. Malware targeting Linux systems frequently exploits misconfigured services, weak SSH credentials, or unpatched vulnerabilities to gain initial access. Once inside, attackers deploy rootkits, cryptojackers, and botnets to establish long-term persistence and execute malicious activities.

Analyzing macOS malware typically begins with examining application bundles and executable files. Since macOS applications use the Mach-O binary format, analysts use tools like otool, nm, and strings to inspect imported libraries, function calls, and embedded strings. Code-signing verification is another important step in macOS malware analysis. Malware developers sometimes use stolen or fraudulent developer certificates to sign their applications, tricking users and bypassing Gatekeeper restrictions. Security researchers use codesign - dvv and spctl --assess to verify the authenticity of macOS binaries and detect tampering.

Dynamic analysis of macOS malware involves monitoring process execution, file system changes, and network activity. Tools like fswatch, fs_usage, and lsof help track file modifications and resource access in real time. Since many macOS malware variants create persistence mechanisms using launch agents, cron jobs, or login items, analysts check /Library/LaunchAgents, /Library/LaunchDaemons, and ~/Library/Preferences for suspicious entries. Monitoring network connections with nettop or lsof -i reveals communication with command-and-control (C2) servers, providing valuable indicators of compromise (IoCs).

MacOS malware often employs obfuscation techniques to evade detection. Attackers use packers, runtime encryption, and shell scripts to conceal malicious payloads. Some macOS malware executes AppleScript commands or leverages system utilities like osascript and curl to download additional components. Analysts use dtruss and fs_usage to trace system calls and identify obfuscated execution flows. Reverse engineering macOS malware requires disassemblers like Hopper or IDA Pro to analyze Mach-O binaries and uncover hidden functionality.

Linux malware analysis follows a similar approach but requires specialized tools for ELF binaries. Since Linux executables use the ELF format, analysts inspect them using readelf, objdump, and strings to identify imported functions and hardcoded data. Malware samples that modify system configurations often target /etc/cron.d, /etc/systemd/system/, and /etc/init.d/ to establish persistence. By checking these directories, analysts can identify unauthorized startup scripts and remove malicious entries.

Many Linux malware variants operate as rootkits, modifying kernel structures to hide processes, files, and network connections. Rootkits such as Suterusu and Diamorphine inject themselves into the kernel, making detection difficult. Analysts use forensic tools like chkrootkit and rkhunter to scan for hidden processes, unauthorized kernel modules, and system anomalies. Live memory analysis with volatility and kernel debugging with gdb provide deeper insights into malware that manipulates system internals.

Cryptojacking malware is a growing concern on Linux systems, as attackers exploit server resources for unauthorized cryptocurrency mining. Malware like Kinsing and WatchDog infect misconfigured Docker containers, deploying mining software that consumes CPU and RAM. These infections often spread through weak SSH credentials, open Docker APIs, or vulnerable web applications. Security teams use htop, ps aux, and netstat -tulnp to identify abnormal resource usage and rogue mining processes. Preventative measures include disabling root login via SSH, enforcing strong passwords, and implementing firewall rules to restrict access to administrative services.

Linux malware often leverages living-off-the-land (LotL) techniques, using legitimate system utilities for malicious purposes. Attackers abuse tools like curl, wget, and bash to execute commands, download payloads, and establish backdoors. Fileless malware variants execute directly in memory, leaving minimal forensic evidence. Analysts use process monitoring tools like auditd, strace, and sysdig to track suspicious activity and identify unusual behavior in running processes.

Advanced Linux malware incorporates evasion techniques such as process hollowing, LD_PRELOAD hijacking, and syscall hooking. Process hollowing allows malware to replace the memory of a legitimate process with its own payload, running undetected under a trusted process name. LD_PRELOAD hijacking manipulates shared libraries to intercept function calls and modify system behavior. Syscall hooking alters system call tables to hide malicious operations from monitoring tools. Analysts use ldd, lsof, and ptrace to detect these evasion methods and analyze modified binaries.

Network-based detection plays a crucial role in identifying macOS and Linux malware infections. Since many threats rely on C2 communication, monitoring outbound connections with tcpdump, Wireshark, or Zeek helps detect unauthorized data exfiltration. Security analysts investigate suspicious DNS requests, encrypted traffic patterns, and unusual outbound connections to identify malware activity. Implementing network segmentation, firewall rules, and intrusion detection systems (IDS) reduces the attack surface and mitigates the spread of malware.

Preventing macOS and Linux malware infections requires a combination of security best practices and proactive monitoring. Organizations should enforce the principle of least privilege, restricting administrative access to minimize the impact of malware. Regular software updates and patch management help eliminate vulnerabilities exploited by attackers. Endpoint detection and response (EDR) solutions provide real-time visibility into system activities, detecting anomalies and blocking malicious behavior.

Security professionals must stay informed about emerging macOS and Linux malware trends, as attackers continuously adapt their techniques. Understanding the unique characteristics of these threats enables analysts to develop effective countermeasures, strengthen defenses, and improve incident response capabilities. By leveraging forensic tools, behavioral analysis, and proactive threat hunting, cybersecurity teams can detect and mitigate macOS and Linux malware before it causes significant damage.

Web-Based Malware and Drive-By Downloads

Web-based malware and drive-by downloads are among the most common and effective methods used by cybercriminals to infect users without requiring direct interaction. These attacks take advantage of vulnerabilities in web browsers, plugins, and operating systems to execute malicious code silently in the background. Drive-by downloads occur when a user visits a compromised or malicious website, triggering an automatic download and execution of malware without the user's knowledge. Web-based malware spreads through exploit kits, malicious advertisements, compromised websites, and deceptive social engineering techniques, making it a persistent threat to both individuals and organizations.

One of the primary attack vectors for web-based malware is malicious websites. Attackers compromise legitimate sites by injecting malicious JavaScript, HTML, or iframe elements that redirect visitors to exploit kits or phishing pages. These injected scripts can execute malicious payloads by exploiting browser vulnerabilities, downloading malware, or stealing user credentials. Websites with weak security configurations, outdated CMS platforms, or vulnerable plugins are common targets for attackers looking to spread malware on a large scale.

Exploit kits are automated frameworks designed to scan a victim's system for vulnerabilities and deliver malware based on detected weaknesses. These kits typically target unpatched browser components, such as Adobe Flash, Java, and outdated versions of Internet Explorer, Chrome, or Firefox. When a user visits a webpage hosting an exploit kit, the kit scans the system for known vulnerabilities and delivers the appropriate malware payload. Notorious exploit kits like Angler, RIG, and Fallout have been used to distribute ransomware, banking trojans, and spyware. As software vendors phase out vulnerable plugins and browsers improve security, exploit kits have declined but still pose a risk to unpatched systems.

Malvertising, or malicious advertising, is another major source of web-based malware infections. Attackers inject malicious code into online ad networks, causing infected ads to appear on legitimate websites. When users view or interact with these ads, they may be redirected to exploit kits, phishing pages, or malware-hosting sites. In some cases, malvertising does not require any user interaction; simply loading a compromised ad in the browser is enough to trigger a drive-by download. Since ad networks distribute content across thousands of websites, a single malvertising campaign can reach millions of users, making it a highly effective malware distribution method.

Social engineering techniques also play a significant role in web-based malware infections. Attackers create fake websites that mimic legitimate banking, social media, or software update pages to deceive users into downloading malware. These fraudulent sites often use domain names similar to the legitimate service, tricking users into entering credentials or installing malicious software. Fake browser update prompts, security warnings, and system alerts are commonly used tactics in these campaigns. Victims who download and execute the suggested files unknowingly install trojans, ransomware, or keyloggers.

Watering hole attacks are another sophisticated form of web-based malware distribution. In these attacks, cybercriminals target specific groups, industries, or organizations by compromising websites that they frequently visit. Instead of attacking users directly, attackers infect a trusted website and wait for their intended victims to visit it. Once a target accesses the compromised site, the malware is delivered through exploit kits or malicious scripts. Watering hole attacks are often used in cyber espionage campaigns, targeting government agencies, defense contractors, and financial institutions.

Browser extensions and add-ons are also exploited as a delivery mechanism for web-based malware. While many extensions provide useful functionality, some are designed to collect user data, inject ads, or redirect users to malicious websites. Attackers often disguise malicious extensions as productivity tools, video downloaders, or security utilities. Once installed, these extensions can modify browser settings, steal login credentials, or inject additional scripts into webpages. Users may unknowingly grant excessive permissions to these extensions, allowing attackers to access browsing history, clipboard data, and even keystrokes.

JavaScript-based malware has become increasingly common in web attacks. Malicious JavaScript code can execute directly within a user's browser, enabling attackers to steal session cookies, track keystrokes, or perform cross-site scripting (XSS) attacks. JavaScript-based malware is often used in formjacking attacks, where attackers inject scripts into payment processing pages to steal credit card information in real time. Magecart is one of the most well-known cybercriminal groups specializing in formjacking attacks, compromising thousands of e-commerce websites globally.

Drive-by downloads can also occur through compromised software distribution channels. Attackers inject malware into software installers, browser plugins, or media players hosted on third-party download sites. Users who download and install these applications unknowingly execute malicious code alongside the legitimate software. Some drive-by downloads exploit file bundling techniques, where adware, spyware, or trojans are included in seemingly harmless applications. Free software download sites, torrent platforms, and unauthorized app stores are common sources of such infections.

Detection and mitigation of web-based malware require a combination of security best practices, software updates, and network monitoring. Users should keep their browsers, plugins, and operating systems updated to patch known vulnerabilities that exploit kits target. Disabling unnecessary plugins such as Flash and Java significantly reduces the attack surface for drive-by downloads. Ad-blocking and script-blocking extensions help prevent malicious ads and scripts from executing within the browser.

Network-level security solutions, such as intrusion detection systems (IDS), domain filtering, and threat intelligence feeds, help detect and block malicious web traffic. Organizations use sandboxing techniques to analyze suspicious links and attachments in isolated environments before allowing access. Security awareness training for employees reduces the risk of falling victim to phishing sites, fake updates, and social engineering tactics.

Forensic analysis of web-based malware involves examining browser history, downloaded files, and network logs for signs of infection. Security analysts use tools like Wireshark, Fiddler, and network forensics platforms to trace malicious connections and identify the source of an infection. Reverse engineering malware samples from drive-by downloads provides insights into attack techniques, helping security teams develop better defenses.

Attackers continuously adapt their methods to bypass security measures, leveraging encrypted communications, fileless techniques, and evasive scripting methods to avoid detection. The rise of web-based malware-as-a-service (MaaS) has enabled even low-skilled cybercriminals to deploy sophisticated attacks with minimal effort. As cyber threats evolve, organizations and individuals must remain vigilant in securing their online activities and implementing proactive defenses against web-based malware and drive-by downloads.

Malicious Office Documents and Macro-Based Threats

Malicious Office documents and macro-based threats have been widely used by cybercriminals to deliver malware, steal credentials, and gain unauthorized access to systems. These threats exploit the trust users place in familiar file formats, such as Microsoft Word, Excel, and PowerPoint, to execute malicious code on a victim's machine. Attackers leverage macros, embedded scripts, and exploits within these documents to bypass security defenses and compromise target systems. As organizations continue to rely on Office files for business operations, the use of malicious documents as an attack vector remains a persistent and evolving threat.

Macros are small scripts written in Visual Basic for Applications (VBA) that automate tasks in Office applications. While macros are designed to improve productivity by automating repetitive functions, cybercriminals use them to execute malicious payloads when an unsuspecting user opens a document. When a victim downloads and opens a malicious Office document, the embedded macro prompts them to enable content, often displaying misleading messages claiming that the document requires macros for proper functionality. If the user enables macros, the malware is executed, typically downloading additional payloads, modifying system settings, or stealing sensitive data.

One of the most common types of macro-based attacks is the use of PowerShell scripts to download and execute malware. Macros invoke PowerShell commands through Shell or WScript.Shell functions, enabling attackers to retrieve and run malicious code from remote servers. Since PowerShell is a legitimate Windows utility, it often bypasses traditional antivirus detection, making it an effective tool for malware distribution. Some macro-based threats employ obfuscation techniques, such as encoding commands in Base64 or splitting strings dynamically, to evade security monitoring tools.

Attackers frequently use social engineering tactics to convince users to open and enable macros in malicious documents. Phishing emails are the primary distribution method, often disguised as invoices, job applications, legal documents, or urgent corporate communications. These emails use urgency, fear, or curiosity to pressure victims into opening attachments without verifying their legitimacy. Some campaigns impersonate well-known organizations or internal employees, making them appear more credible.

Embedded exploits in Office documents represent another significant attack vector. Instead of relying on macros, some malicious documents exploit vulnerabilities in Microsoft Office or related components, such as Equation Editor, to execute arbitrary code. These exploits are often delivered as specially crafted .doc, .xls, or .ppt files that trigger a buffer overflow or remote code execution vulnerability when opened. Attackers use these exploits to gain initial access to a system, install backdoors, or deploy reconnaissance tools for further attacks.

Excel 4.0 macros (XLM macros) have seen a resurgence in recent years, as they provide an alternative method for executing malicious code. Unlike VBA macros, which are more commonly monitored and restricted, XLM macros operate at a lower level within Excel's functionality. Cybercriminals use XLM macros to execute shell commands, download payloads, and manipulate registry settings. Since many security tools focus on detecting VBA-based threats, XLM-based attacks often evade detection.

Persistence mechanisms in macro-based malware allow threats to maintain access to a system even after a reboot or user logout. Some macro-based malware modifies registry keys to execute scripts at startup, while others use scheduled tasks or create malicious LNK (shortcut) files to re-launch the attack. Advanced variants inject code into legitimate processes, making them more difficult to detect and remove.

Financial malware and banking trojans often leverage macro-based threats to steal login credentials and authentication tokens. Malware families such as Emotet, TrickBot, and Dridex have historically used malicious Office documents as their primary infection vector. These threats steal sensitive financial data, exfiltrate documents, and deliver secondary payloads, such as ransomware or remote access trojans (RATs).

Sandbox evasion techniques are commonly incorporated into macro-based threats to avoid detection in controlled environments. Some malicious macros check system properties, such as CPU model, RAM size, or username, to determine whether they are running in a sandbox. If suspicious conditions are detected, the malware terminates execution to prevent analysis. Other evasion techniques include delaying execution, requiring user interaction (such as clicking a button), or detecting the presence of security monitoring tools.

Mitigation strategies against macro-based threats involve a combination of security controls and user awareness. Organizations should disable macros by default and implement policies that prevent users from enabling them unless necessary. Office security settings, such as Protected View and Macro Security, should be configured to block potentially harmful macros from running automatically. Email filtering solutions help detect and block malicious attachments before they reach users, reducing the likelihood of infection.

Behavior-based detection is essential for identifying malicious macros that use obfuscation techniques to evade traditional antivirus solutions. Endpoint detection and response (EDR) tools monitor process activity, API calls, and PowerShell execution patterns to detect suspicious behavior. Network monitoring solutions track outbound connections to known malicious domains or IP addresses used by macro-based malware for command-and-control (C2) communications.

Security awareness training is crucial in preventing macro-based attacks, as social engineering remains the primary method of distributing malicious Office documents. Employees should be educated on recognizing phishing emails, verifying document sources before opening attachments, and reporting suspicious activity. Organizations should conduct regular phishing simulations to reinforce best practices and improve user resilience against social engineering attacks.

Threat intelligence sharing among security professionals helps identify emerging macro-based threats and develop effective countermeasures. Cybersecurity organizations and vendors provide indicators of compromise (IoCs) related to known campaigns, enabling security teams to proactively block malicious documents and associated infrastructure. Continuous monitoring of malware trends ensures that defenses remain up to date against evolving attack techniques.

MacOS and Linux systems are not entirely immune to malicious Office documents, as attackers increasingly develop cross-platform threats. MacOS users face risks from macro-based malware that executes AppleScript commands or abuses system utilities like osascript and curl. Linux-based attacks leverage malicious LibreOffice or OpenOffice documents to execute shell scripts and gain access to user accounts. Although these platforms have additional security layers, users should remain cautious when opening Office files from untrusted sources.

As cybercriminals refine their techniques, macro-based threats continue to pose a significant risk to organizations and individuals. Attackers leverage document-based exploits, obfuscation methods, and social engineering tactics to bypass security defenses and infect systems. By implementing robust security controls, educating users, and leveraging advanced threat detection tools, organizations can mitigate the risks associated with malicious Office documents and macro-based attacks.

Email-Based Malware and Phishing Campaigns

Email-based malware and phishing campaigns remain among the most effective attack vectors used by cybercriminals to infiltrate organizations, steal sensitive information, and spread malicious software. Despite advancements in security technologies, email continues to be a major entry point for malware infections due to human error and social engineering tactics. Attackers exploit trust, urgency, and deception to convince users to click on malicious links, open infected attachments, or provide credentials. Understanding the techniques used in email-based malware distribution and phishing campaigns is essential for improving detection and mitigation strategies.

Phishing attacks typically involve fraudulent emails designed to trick recipients into revealing login credentials, financial information, or other sensitive data. These emails often impersonate trusted entities such as banks, government agencies, cloud service providers, or internal company departments. Attackers use tactics like domain spoofing, brand impersonation, and urgent messaging to create a sense of legitimacy. Once a victim clicks on a malicious link, they are redirected to a fake login page that captures their credentials and sends them to the attacker. Some phishing emails contain malicious attachments that install malware upon opening.

Spear phishing is a more targeted form of phishing that focuses on specific individuals, organizations, or industries. Unlike generic phishing campaigns, spear phishing emails are carefully crafted based on reconnaissance of the target. Attackers research their victims using publicly available information, social media, or previous data breaches to create personalized messages. These emails often appear to come from colleagues, executives, or business partners, making them more convincing. Spear phishing is commonly used in corporate espionage, financial fraud, and nation-state cyber operations.

Business Email Compromise (BEC) is a sophisticated phishing tactic where attackers impersonate high-ranking executives, suppliers, or employees to manipulate victims into transferring funds or sharing confidential information. BEC attacks typically do not involve malware but rely entirely on social engineering. Attackers often compromise legitimate email accounts through credential theft and use them to send fraudulent requests to finance departments or business partners. Since BEC emails originate from real accounts, they often bypass traditional spam filters and security controls.

Email-based malware delivery relies on attachments, embedded links, and exploit techniques to infect recipients. Malicious attachments come in various formats, including Word documents, Excel spreadsheets, PDFs, ZIP files, and executable files. Attackers embed macros, scripts, or exploits in these attachments, which execute malicious code when the user opens the file. Common malware families distributed through email attachments include banking trojans, ransomware, spyware, and remote access trojans (RATs).

Embedded links in phishing emails often lead to malicious websites that host exploit kits, credential harvesting forms, or fake software downloads. Attackers use domain spoofing and typosquatting to make URLs appear legitimate. Some phishing campaigns employ URL shorteners or obfuscation techniques to hide the true destination of links. Advanced phishing kits generate convincing fake login pages that mimic real services, making it difficult for users to distinguish between legitimate and malicious sites.

Malware delivered through email frequently uses evasion techniques to bypass security defenses. Attackers encrypt or compress payloads to prevent detection by email scanners. Some malware variants employ multi-stage delivery, where the initial attachment contains only a downloader that retrieves the actual payload from a remote server. Obfuscation techniques, such as embedding malicious scripts in images or using HTML smuggling, make it harder for security tools to analyze and block threats.

Ransomware attacks often begin with phishing emails containing malicious attachments or links to infected websites. Once executed, the ransomware encrypts files on the victim's system and demands payment for decryption. Some ransomware campaigns, such as those using Emotet and TrickBot, employ botnets to distribute payloads through massive email spam campaigns. Attackers constantly evolve their tactics, using new lures, encryption techniques, and distribution methods to increase infection rates.

Credential harvesting is a primary objective of many phishing campaigns. Stolen login credentials grant attackers access to email accounts, corporate networks, cloud services, and financial accounts. Once an attacker gains access to an email account, they can use it to launch further attacks, steal sensitive data, or impersonate the victim in social engineering schemes. Credential stuffing attacks, where stolen passwords are tested against multiple accounts, often follow successful phishing campaigns.

Detection and prevention of email-based malware and phishing require a multi-layered security approach. Organizations should implement secure email gateways (SEGs) that filter out phishing emails, scan attachments for malware, and block malicious URLs. Advanced threat detection solutions use machine learning and behavior analysis to identify suspicious email patterns and prevent phishing attempts. Email authentication protocols such as SPF, DKIM, and DMARC help prevent domain spoofing and reduce the effectiveness of impersonation attacks.

User awareness and training play a crucial role in mitigating email-based threats. Employees should be educated on recognizing phishing emails, verifying sender identities, and avoiding clicking on unknown links or attachments. Simulated phishing exercises help organizations assess user susceptibility to phishing attacks and reinforce security best practices. Implementing multi-factor authentication (MFA) adds an extra layer of protection, making it more difficult for attackers to exploit stolen credentials.

Incident response to phishing and email-based malware infections involves rapid detection, containment, and remediation. Security teams should monitor email logs, flag suspicious login attempts, and investigate reported phishing emails. If a phishing attack is successful, compromised accounts should be locked down, passwords reset, and affected systems scanned for malware. Threat intelligence sharing with industry peers and cybersecurity organizations helps organizations stay informed about emerging phishing techniques and malware campaigns.

Email remains one of the most exploited attack vectors due to human vulnerability and the widespread use of email communication in business operations. Cybercriminals continuously refine their tactics, leveraging automation, artificial intelligence, and deepfake technologies to make phishing emails more convincing. Security teams must stay vigilant, adapt their defenses, and educate users to reduce the risk of email-based malware and phishing attacks.

Social Engineering and Malware Distribution

Social engineering is a psychological manipulation technique used by cybercriminals to deceive individuals into divulging sensitive information, downloading malware, or granting unauthorized access to systems. Unlike traditional cyberattacks that rely on technical exploits, social engineering attacks exploit human behavior, trust, and cognitive biases. Malware distribution through social engineering remains one of the most effective tactics for cybercriminals, as users often bypass security measures when they believe they are interacting with a legitimate source. Understanding social engineering techniques and how they facilitate malware distribution is critical in defending against modern cyber threats.

One of the most common methods of social engineering used to distribute malware is phishing. Phishing attacks involve fraudulent emails, messages, or websites that impersonate legitimate organizations, tricking users into opening malicious attachments or clicking on harmful links. These emails often contain urgent requests, such as account verification notices, security warnings, or financial updates, to pressure the recipient into taking immediate action. Once the user interacts with the phishing content, malware is silently installed on their device, leading to credential theft, system compromise, or financial fraud.

Spear phishing is a more targeted form of phishing, focusing on specific individuals, businesses, or government entities. Cybercriminals research their targets using publicly available information, social media, or previous data breaches to craft highly convincing messages. Spear phishing emails may appear to come from a trusted colleague, supplier, or senior executive, making them more difficult to detect. These attacks often deliver malware that establishes a foothold within corporate networks, allowing attackers to conduct espionage, financial fraud, or ransomware attacks.

Whaling attacks are a specialized form of spear phishing that targets high-profile individuals such as executives, government officials, or business leaders. Since these individuals often have access to sensitive information and financial resources, attackers craft highly sophisticated emails designed to bypass traditional security filters. Whaling emails may impersonate legal or financial documents, requesting wire transfers, login credentials, or access to internal systems. Malware delivered through whaling attacks can provide attackers with long-term access to an organization's infrastructure, leading to large-scale breaches.

Another widely used social engineering tactic for malware distribution is baiting. Baiting involves luring victims into downloading malware by offering something enticing, such as free software, music, movies, or security updates. Attackers often host malware-infected files on pirated content websites, torrent platforms, or fraudulent software download pages. Once downloaded, the malware executes in the background, stealing information, installing additional payloads, or compromising system integrity. Baiting attacks take advantage of users' curiosity and willingness to download free content without verifying its source.

Pretexting is another social engineering method used to distribute malware. In a pretexting attack, the attacker creates a fabricated scenario to manipulate the target into revealing information or performing actions that compromise security. This can include impersonating IT support personnel, law enforcement officers, or banking representatives to trick victims into installing remote access tools or providing sensitive credentials. Once the attacker gains access, they deploy malware such as keyloggers, trojans, or ransomware to exploit the compromised system.

Scareware is a form of social engineering that tricks users into believing their computer is infected with malware, prompting them to install fraudulent security software. Scareware campaigns rely on fake pop-up alerts, misleading website banners, or deceptive phone calls claiming to offer technical support. When users download the suggested software, they often install actual malware that steals data, encrypts files, or grants attackers remote control over the device. Some scareware variants demand payment for fake antivirus services, making them a form of financial fraud.

Malvertising, or malicious advertising, is another social engineering technique used to distribute malware. Attackers inject malicious code into online advertisements that appear on legitimate websites. When users view or click on the ad, they may be redirected to a phishing site, tricked into downloading a fake software update, or exposed to exploit kits that silently install malware. Since advertising networks distribute content across multiple websites, malvertising campaigns can reach a vast number of users, spreading malware on a large scale.

Cybercriminals also use social media as a platform for social engineering attacks and malware distribution. Fake social media profiles, impersonated company accounts, and deceptive messages are used to spread malicious links and attachments. Attackers may pose as friends, colleagues, or customer support representatives to gain victims' trust and convince them to execute malware. Malicious links embedded in social media posts, direct messages, or comments often lead to phishing sites or exploit-laden downloads.

QR code phishing, also known as quishing, is an emerging social engineering tactic used to spread malware. Attackers create fraudulent QR codes that, when scanned, redirect users to malicious websites or automatically download malware onto their mobile devices. Since users are often less cautious with QR codes than traditional links, quishing bypasses many conventional phishing defenses. Attackers distribute malicious QR codes through phishing emails, fake advertisements, or even printed materials in public places.

Voice phishing (vishing) and SMS phishing (smishing) are additional social engineering techniques used to manipulate victims into installing malware. Vishing attacks involve fraudulent phone calls where attackers impersonate customer support agents, IT staff, or financial institutions, convincing victims to download remote access tools or provide sensitive information. Smishing, on the other hand, uses deceptive text messages that contain malicious links or instructions to install malware. These attacks exploit users' trust in mobile communication and often bypass traditional email security measures.

Cybercriminals frequently combine multiple social engineering tactics to increase their chances of success. A phishing email may include a malicious attachment and a follow-up phone call to reinforce its legitimacy. Fake job offers may lure victims into opening infected resumes, while fraudulent invoices convince employees to execute macro-enabled documents that install malware. By adapting their methods based on the target's behavior and industry, attackers maximize their effectiveness and bypass security defenses.

Defending against social engineering attacks requires a combination of technological solutions, security policies, and user awareness. Organizations should implement strong email filtering, endpoint protection, and web security controls to detect and block malicious content. Multi-factor authentication (MFA) reduces the impact of credential theft by requiring additional verification before granting access. Regular security training programs help employees recognize phishing attempts, avoid clicking on suspicious links, and verify requests before taking action.

Incident response and threat intelligence sharing play a crucial role in mitigating social engineering-based malware distribution. Security teams should continuously monitor for suspicious activity, investigate reported phishing attempts, and implement proactive defenses against emerging threats. Threat intelligence platforms help organizations stay informed about new social engineering tactics, malware variants, and attacker trends. By analyzing attack patterns and collaborating with industry peers, cybersecurity professionals can develop more effective countermeasures.

Social engineering remains one of the most dangerous and adaptable methods of malware distribution. As technology evolves, attackers refine their techniques to exploit human psychology and trust. Organizations and individuals must remain vigilant, continuously educating themselves on the latest threats and implementing strong security measures to defend against the ever-evolving landscape of social engineering and malware attacks.

Threat Intelligence and Malware Attribution

Threat intelligence and malware attribution are critical components of modern cybersecurity, helping organizations identify, track, and defend against malicious actors. Threat intelligence involves collecting and analyzing data on cyber threats to enhance an organization's ability to prevent, detect, and respond to attacks. Malware attribution, on the other hand, focuses on determining the origin, motivation, and methods of a particular cyber threat. Together, these disciplines provide security teams with the insights needed to anticipate attacks, improve defensive strategies, and contribute to broader efforts in cybercrime prevention.

Threat intelligence is categorized into three main types: tactical, operational, and strategic intelligence. Tactical threat intelligence focuses on immediate, actionable information, such as indicators of compromise (IoCs), IP addresses, domains, hashes, and signatures associated with known malware. Security teams use this data to detect and block threats in real time, integrating it into firewalls, intrusion detection systems (IDS), and endpoint security solutions. Tactical intelligence is often shared among organizations and cybersecurity communities to strengthen collective defenses against emerging threats.

Operational threat intelligence provides deeper insights into the techniques, tactics, and procedures (TTPs) used by cybercriminals and advanced persistent threat (APT) groups. By analyzing attack patterns, malware behaviors, and exploit methods, security professionals gain a better understanding of how attackers operate. This level of intelligence helps in identifying trends, predicting future threats, and developing countermeasures tailored to specific attack methodologies. Operational intelligence is crucial for incident response teams, enabling them to correlate attacks and determine whether they are part of a larger campaign.

Strategic threat intelligence focuses on the broader geopolitical and economic factors influencing cyber threats. This type of intelligence helps organizations and government agencies assess the risks posed by nation-state actors, cybercriminal syndicates, and hacktivist groups. Strategic intelligence informs high-level decision-making, shaping cybersecurity policies, investment strategies, and risk management frameworks. It involves analyzing motivations behind cyber attacks, such as financial gain, espionage, political influence, or disruption of critical infrastructure.

Malware attribution is the process of identifying the individuals, groups, or organizations responsible for a cyber attack. Attribution is challenging because attackers use sophisticated evasion techniques to disguise their origins. Cybercriminals often route attacks through multiple countries, use anonymization tools like Tor, and employ false flags to mislead investigators. Despite these challenges, cybersecurity experts use a combination of forensic analysis, threat intelligence, and behavioral profiling to attribute attacks to specific actors.

One of the key methods used in malware attribution is code similarity analysis. By comparing malware samples to previously identified threats, researchers can determine whether a new attack is related to known threat actors. Similarities in coding style, encryption routines, command-and-control (C2) infrastructure, and execution methods provide valuable clues about the origins of a malware strain. Some threat groups reuse components from past campaigns, making it possible to link attacks over time.

Network analysis also plays a crucial role in attribution. Investigators track the infrastructure used by attackers, including IP addresses, domain registrations, and C2 servers. While cybercriminals frequently change their infrastructure to avoid detection, persistent patterns in hosting providers, domain naming conventions, and encryption keys can reveal connections between attacks. Threat intelligence platforms collect and correlate this data, allowing security researchers to attribute malware to specific groups or geographic regions.

Language analysis is another technique used in malware attribution. Attackers often leave linguistic traces in malware code, phishing emails, and C2 communications. By analyzing grammar, syntax, and word choices, researchers can identify regional language patterns and potential national origins. Some cybercriminal groups use machine translations or deliberately insert misleading phrases to obscure their identities, but careful linguistic analysis can still provide attribution insights.

Threat actor profiling involves studying the motivations, targets, and historical activities of known cybercriminal groups. Certain APT groups consistently target government agencies, defense contractors, or financial institutions, while others focus on ransomware, fraud, or industrial espionage. By mapping out an attacker's objectives and preferred attack methods, security teams can attribute incidents to specific adversaries. Attribution reports from cybersecurity firms, law enforcement agencies, and intelligence organizations contribute to this knowledge base.

Attribution efforts often involve collaboration between private security companies, government agencies, and international organizations. Cybercrime investigations require cooperation across jurisdictions, as attacks frequently span multiple countries. Organizations like INTERPOL, Europol, and the FBI work with cybersecurity researchers to track and dismantle cybercriminal networks. Attribution findings can lead to sanctions, arrests, or counter-cyber operations designed to disrupt threat actors' activities.

Despite the importance of attribution, it is not always necessary for effective cybersecurity defense. While identifying an attacker can provide valuable insights, organizations primarily focus on mitigating threats and preventing future attacks. Security teams prioritize threat intelligence that enables them to detect, block, and respond to malware rather than spending excessive resources on attribution. However, in cases involving nation-state actors, financial crime syndicates, or ransomware groups, attribution becomes critical for legal, political, and counterintelligence purposes.

Cybercriminals continue to evolve their tactics, making attribution increasingly difficult. Some attackers use malware-as-a-service (MaaS) platforms, where multiple groups deploy the same malware, complicating efforts to link attacks to a single source. Others employ deception techniques, such as using stolen credentials or compromised infrastructure, to create false attribution trails. As a result, threat intelligence analysts must rely on multiple data points, cross-referencing evidence from various sources to reach reliable conclusions.

The rise of artificial intelligence (AI) and machine learning in threat intelligence has improved attribution capabilities. AI-driven analysis can process vast amounts of threat data, identifying patterns that human analysts might miss. Machine learning models help detect anomalies in network traffic, correlate malware samples, and predict emerging attack trends. By automating parts of the attribution process, AI enhances the speed and accuracy of threat intelligence efforts.

Threat intelligence sharing among organizations is vital for strengthening collective security. Cybersecurity information-sharing alliances, such as the Cyber Threat Alliance (CTA) and Information Sharing and Analysis Centers (ISACs), enable organizations to exchange threat intelligence in real time. By sharing malware indicators, attack signatures, and attribution findings, security teams can better defend against known threats and anticipate future attacks.

Threat intelligence and malware attribution are essential tools in the fight against cyber threats. By collecting, analyzing, and sharing threat data, organizations improve their ability to detect and respond to attacks. While attribution remains a challenging and complex process, advancements in forensic analysis, AI-driven threat detection, and international cooperation continue to enhance the accuracy and effectiveness of cyber investigations. Understanding the motivations, tactics, and infrastructure of threat actors helps security professionals develop proactive defense strategies, reducing the overall impact of cybercrime on businesses and society.

YARA Rules and Malware Classification

YARA is a powerful tool used for malware classification and threat hunting, enabling security researchers and analysts to identify, categorize, and detect malicious files based on specific patterns. It provides a flexible and efficient way to write detection rules that match known malware samples or variants, helping organizations strengthen their cybersecurity defenses. YARA rules use textual and binary pattern-matching techniques to classify malware into families, detect new variants, and assist in forensic investigations. As malware evolves and becomes more sophisticated, YARA plays a crucial role in threat intelligence and automated malware detection.

YARA rules consist of structured patterns that define the characteristics of a malware sample. Each rule contains a set of conditions that must be met for a file to be classified as malicious. These conditions include string patterns, hexadecimal sequences, metadata, and logical expressions that match specific traits of known malware. Analysts create rules based on static and behavioral attributes of malware, allowing security tools to scan files, memory, and network traffic for threats. By continuously updating YARA rules, cybersecurity teams can detect newly emerging threats while minimizing false positives.

A basic YARA rule contains three main sections: metadata, strings, and conditions. The metadata section includes information about the rule, such as its author, date, and a description of the malware it detects. The strings section defines specific text or binary patterns found in the malware sample, including hardcoded URLs, function names, encryption keys, or error messages. The conditions section specifies the logical criteria that determine whether a file matches the defined patterns. Rules can be fine-tuned using Boolean operators, regular expressions, and count-based conditions to increase detection accuracy.

Malware classification using YARA relies on pattern recognition techniques to differentiate between various malware families. Security researchers analyze malware samples to identify unique code segments, behavioral signatures, and file structures that distinguish one variant from another. By grouping similar malware samples, analysts can map the evolution of a malware strain, track adversary tactics, and anticipate future threats. Classification helps incident response teams respond more effectively to infections by applying the appropriate remediation strategies based on the malware family.

One of the key benefits of YARA rules is their ability to detect polymorphic and metamorphic malware. Traditional signature-based detection methods often fail against these types of threats because the malware changes its code structure while maintaining its core functionality. YARA rules address this challenge by searching for specific patterns in obfuscated or encrypted payloads. Analysts use wildcard characters, regular expressions, and partial byte sequences to detect malware that modifies itself dynamically to evade security tools.

YARA rules are widely used in malware sandboxing and automated analysis environments. Security platforms integrate YARA into sandbox systems to analyze files in real time, identifying threats before they reach enterprise networks. When a suspicious file is executed in a sandbox, YARA rules scan the memory, network activity, and file system changes to detect known malicious behaviors. This automated approach accelerates threat detection, reduces manual analysis workload, and improves the efficiency of security operations.

Advanced malware detection with YARA includes the use of contextual and behavioral indicators. Instead of relying solely on static string matching, analysts create rules that consider execution flow, API calls, registry modifications, and network communications. These behavioral rules improve detection accuracy by identifying malware based on its actions rather than its static attributes. By correlating multiple indicators, YARA rules enhance the ability to detect malware variants that attempt to bypass traditional defenses.

Cybercriminals continuously develop evasion techniques to defeat YARA-based detection. Some malware authors use encryption, obfuscation, and packing methods to hide malicious code from static analysis. Others implement anti-analysis techniques that detect whether a file is being scanned and modify its behavior accordingly. To counter these strategies, security researchers create heuristic-based YARA rules that focus on malware characteristics that are difficult to conceal, such as execution patterns, entropy levels, and system API usage.

YARA is also used in threat hunting operations, where security teams proactively search for malware indicators across enterprise networks. Threat hunters deploy YARA rules in security information and event management (SIEM) systems, intrusion detection systems (IDS), and endpoint detection and response (EDR) tools to scan for signs of compromise. By analyzing log data, memory dumps, and network packets, organizations can identify hidden infections and take preventive action before a full-scale attack occurs.

Integration of YARA with forensic analysis tools enhances incident response capabilities. Security professionals use YARA to analyze disk images, memory snapshots, and suspicious file samples collected from compromised systems. By matching forensic artifacts against known threat signatures, investigators can reconstruct attack timelines, identify the initial infection vector, and determine the full scope of a breach. This intelligence helps organizations strengthen their defenses and improve their response strategies for future incidents.

YARA is widely adopted across the cybersecurity community, with researchers continuously contributing new rules to public repositories. Platforms like VirusTotal, MISP, and GitHub host collections of YARA rules developed by security experts, enabling organizations to leverage collective threat intelligence. Open-source YARA rule-sharing initiatives enhance global cybersecurity efforts by providing real-time updates on emerging threats and new malware strains. Collaboration among security professionals ensures that detection capabilities remain ahead of adversary tactics.

Despite its strengths, YARA has limitations that security analysts must consider. False positives can occur when rules are too broad, flagging legitimate files as malware. Conversely, overly restrictive rules may fail to detect certain threats. Analysts must balance rule sensitivity and specificity, regularly testing and refining detection criteria to maintain accuracy. Performance impact is another factor, as scanning large datasets with complex YARA rules can consume significant system resources. Optimization techniques, such as rule consolidation and selective scanning, help mitigate performance issues.

The future of YARA and malware classification continues to evolve with advancements in machine learning and artificial intelligence (AI). Researchers are exploring AI-driven approaches to generate YARA rules automatically based on malware behavior patterns. These techniques enhance detection efficiency, reduce the reliance on manual rule creation, and improve adaptability to emerging threats. AI-powered YARA integration enables faster identification of zero-day malware and more accurate classification of new threat families.

YARA remains a foundational tool in malware analysis, classification, and threat hunting. Its flexible rule-based approach allows security professionals to detect known and emerging threats effectively. By combining static and behavioral detection techniques, YARA enhances cybersecurity defenses and provides organizations with proactive threat intelligence. Continuous updates, collaborative rule-sharing, and integration with advanced security solutions ensure that YARA remains a vital component in the fight against malware.

Using Sandboxes for Malware Analysis

Malware analysis is a critical process in cybersecurity, helping security researchers and incident responders understand the behavior, functionality, and impact of malicious software. One of the most effective techniques for analyzing malware is the use of sandboxes—

controlled, isolated environments where malicious code can be executed safely without affecting the host system. Sandboxes provide a secure way to observe malware behavior in real time, identify indicators of compromise (IoCs), and develop detection mechanisms. By leveraging sandboxing techniques, analysts can detect and neutralize threats before they cause significant damage.

A sandbox is a virtualized or isolated environment that mimics a real operating system, allowing malware to execute while preventing it from interacting with the actual system. Sandboxes are designed to capture and log the actions of malicious files, including process creation, registry modifications, file system changes, network connections, and API calls. This analysis provides valuable insights into how malware operates, what data it targets, and whether it attempts to evade detection.

There are two primary types of sandboxes used in malware analysis: dynamic and static sandboxes. Dynamic sandboxes execute malware in a live environment, monitoring its behavior in real time. They provide detailed reports on the malware's actions, helping analysts identify malicious patterns and determine its purpose. Static sandboxes, on the other hand, analyze malware without execution, focusing on file structure, embedded strings, and code signatures. While static analysis can identify known threats quickly, dynamic analysis is essential for detecting polymorphic and fileless malware that modifies itself during execution.

Sandboxing is particularly useful for analyzing zero-day malware, which exploits previously unknown vulnerabilities. Since traditional antivirus and signature-based detection methods often fail to recognize new threats, sandboxes play a crucial role in uncovering malware behaviors that have not yet been documented. By executing suspicious files in a sandbox, analysts can determine whether they exhibit malicious characteristics, even if no prior signatures exist for them.

One of the key advantages of sandboxing is its ability to capture network activity generated by malware. Many modern threats communicate with command-and-control (C2) servers to receive instructions, exfiltrate data, or download additional payloads.

Sandboxes monitor these connections, logging details such as destination IP addresses, domains, and encryption methods used by the malware. This information helps security teams block malicious infrastructure and create firewall rules to prevent further infections.

Malware developers continuously evolve their techniques to evade detection by sandboxes. Some malware samples include environment checks to determine whether they are running in a virtualized or controlled environment. If the malware detects a sandbox, it may alter its behavior, delay execution, or terminate itself to avoid analysis. Common evasion techniques include checking system uptime, detecting virtual machine (VM) artifacts, querying hardware configurations, and monitoring for analysis tools running in the background.

To counteract these evasion tactics, security researchers use advanced sandboxing techniques that mimic real user behavior. This includes simulating mouse movements, keyboard interactions, and normal system activity to convince malware that it is running on an actual user's machine. Some sandboxes employ VM cloaking techniques to hide virtualization artifacts, preventing malware from recognizing that it is being analyzed. These methods improve the effectiveness of sandboxing by allowing analysts to observe malware behavior without triggering its self-defense mechanisms.

Automated malware analysis platforms integrate sandboxing to streamline threat detection and response. Security solutions such as Cuckoo Sandbox, Any.Run, Joe Sandbox, and FireEye's Dynamic Threat Intelligence provide real-time malware analysis using sandboxing technologies. These platforms generate detailed reports on malware behavior, allowing security teams to quickly assess threats and take action. Many enterprise security systems also integrate sandboxing into email gateways, endpoint protection solutions, and network security appliances to automatically detect and block malicious files before they reach users.

Behavioral analysis in sandboxes helps categorize malware into families based on their actions. For example, ransomware exhibits characteristic behaviors such as encrypting files, modifying file extensions, and displaying ransom notes. Banking trojans inject code into web browsers, capture keystrokes, and attempt to steal authentication credentials. By recognizing these behavior patterns, security analysts can classify malware accurately and develop effective countermeasures.

Sandboxing also plays a key role in incident response and forensic investigations. When a system is compromised, security teams use sandboxes to analyze malicious files found on the affected machine. By executing these files in a controlled environment, analysts can reconstruct the attack chain, identify patient zero, and determine whether additional systems are at risk. This forensic analysis helps organizations understand the full scope of a security breach and implement measures to prevent future incidents.

Organizations implementing sandboxing solutions must consider performance and scalability. Running malware in a sandbox requires system resources, and large-scale enterprises may need high-performance analysis environments to process multiple files simultaneously. Cloud-based sandboxes offer scalability, allowing organizations to analyze malware samples without deploying additional hardware. However, on-premise sandboxes provide greater control over data privacy and security, making them ideal for organizations handling sensitive information.

Despite its effectiveness, sandboxing is not a standalone solution for malware detection. Attackers constantly develop new techniques to bypass sandbox analysis, including multi-stage execution, encrypted payloads, and user interaction dependencies. To enhance malware detection, organizations combine sandboxing with threat intelligence, machine learning, and heuristic analysis. By correlating sandbox results with real-world attack data, security teams improve their ability to detect and respond to emerging threats.

As malware continues to evolve, sandboxing remains a vital tool in the cybersecurity arsenal. It provides a safe and efficient way to analyze malicious files, detect zero-day threats, and understand attacker tactics. By leveraging advanced sandboxing techniques and integrating them with broader security strategies, organizations strengthen their defenses against sophisticated malware campaigns.

Network Traffic Analysis for Malware Detection

Network traffic analysis is a crucial technique for detecting and mitigating malware infections. Since malware often relies on network communication for command-and-control (C2) operations, data exfiltration, and lateral movement, monitoring network traffic provides valuable insights into malicious activity. By analyzing network packets, flow patterns, and anomalous connections, security teams can identify malware infections that may otherwise go undetected by traditional endpoint security measures. Network traffic analysis helps organizations detect compromised systems, block malicious communications, and respond to cyber threats more effectively.

Malware generates different types of network traffic depending on its purpose and functionality. Many malware variants establish connections with remote C2 servers to receive instructions, update payloads, or exfiltrate stolen data. Others use peer-to-peer (P2P) communication to avoid centralized detection. Some malware families leverage domain generation algorithms (DGA) to create random domain names dynamically, preventing security tools from blocking them based on static blacklists. Understanding these traffic patterns allows analysts to develop detection rules that identify malicious activity in real time.

One of the primary indicators of malware-related network traffic is unusual outbound connections. Many malware infections generate connections to suspicious IP addresses or domains that are not typically accessed by legitimate applications. Security analysts monitor outbound traffic for connections to known malicious servers, unusual geographic locations, or encrypted communication tunnels that deviate from normal network behavior. Intrusion detection systems

(IDS) and intrusion prevention systems (IPS) play a key role in identifying these anomalies and blocking malicious traffic before it can cause harm.

DNS analysis is an effective method for detecting malware that relies on domain-based C2 communication. Malware often uses DNS queries to resolve domain names associated with its C2 infrastructure. By monitoring DNS request patterns, analysts can identify suspicious domain resolutions, high-frequency DNS lookups, or requests to newly registered domains. Threat intelligence feeds provide lists of known malicious domains, allowing security teams to correlate DNS queries with known threat indicators. Additionally, detecting randomized or algorithmically generated domain names can help identify malware using DGA-based evasion techniques.

Encrypted traffic analysis is another important aspect of malware detection. Many modern malware variants use SSL/TLS encryption to hide their network communications from security monitoring tools. While encryption prevents direct inspection of packet contents, analysts can still identify malicious behavior by analyzing metadata such as SSL certificates, handshake patterns, and traffic volume. Anomalies such as self-signed certificates, expired certificate authorities, or TLS connections to suspicious IP addresses often indicate malware activity. Deep packet inspection (DPI) and SSL interception techniques help uncover hidden threats within encrypted network traffic.

Beaconing behavior is a common characteristic of malware communicating with a C2 server. Many malware variants establish periodic connections to their C2 infrastructure, sending small heartbeat signals to indicate that the infected machine is still active. These beaconing patterns often follow predictable intervals, making them detectable through network traffic analysis. Security analysts use network flow analysis tools to identify repeated outbound connections with similar time intervals, which may indicate the presence of botnets, remote access trojans (RATs), or spyware.

Lateral movement detection is another critical use case for network traffic analysis. Once malware compromises a system, it often attempts to spread within the network by exploiting open ports, weak credentials, or unpatched vulnerabilities. Network monitoring tools detect suspicious internal connections, such as unauthorized remote desktop protocol (RDP) sessions, excessive file transfers via SMB, or unusual SSH login attempts. By tracking these activities, security teams can contain malware infections before they escalate into widespread breaches.

Exfiltration detection is essential for preventing data theft by malware. Many information-stealing malware variants attempt to extract sensitive data, such as login credentials, financial records, or intellectual property, from compromised systems. Data exfiltration techniques include uploading stolen files to external FTP or HTTP servers, sending encrypted payloads over DNS tunneling, or hiding data within normal-looking network requests. Network traffic analysis tools identify large outbound data transfers, unauthorized file uploads, or abnormal bandwidth usage, helping organizations prevent data breaches caused by malware infections.

Threat hunting using network traffic analysis enables security teams to proactively identify malware infections that may have bypassed traditional security controls. By searching for patterns associated with known malware behaviors, analysts can uncover hidden infections, investigate suspicious traffic flows, and isolate compromised devices. Threat hunting methodologies involve correlating network activity with threat intelligence sources, analyzing network flow anomalies, and conducting retrospective analysis of past traffic logs to identify undetected threats.

Automated detection solutions integrate machine learning and artificial intelligence (AI) to enhance network traffic analysis for malware detection. AI-driven security tools analyze vast amounts of network data, identifying deviations from normal behavior that may indicate malware activity. Machine learning algorithms detect emerging threats by recognizing traffic patterns associated with malware variants, even if no prior signatures exist. Behavioral analysis models help differentiate between legitimate network activity and malicious communications, improving the accuracy of malware detection.

Security information and event management (SIEM) systems play a key role in correlating network traffic analysis with other security data sources. SIEM platforms aggregate logs from firewalls, IDS/IPS, DNS servers, and endpoint protection systems, allowing security teams to detect coordinated attack campaigns. By integrating network traffic data with endpoint forensics, SIEM solutions provide a comprehensive view of malware activity across an organization's infrastructure. Automated alerting mechanisms notify security teams of potential threats, enabling faster response times and incident containment.

Challenges in network traffic analysis for malware detection include the increasing volume of encrypted traffic, the use of legitimate cloud services for malware hosting, and the complexity of distinguishing between normal and malicious activity. Cybercriminals use techniques such as domain fronting, obfuscation, and traffic tunneling to evade detection. To counter these tactics, security teams employ a combination of anomaly detection, signature-based filtering, and real-time network monitoring. Continuous updates to threat intelligence databases ensure that security tools remain effective against evolving malware threats.

Organizations implementing network traffic analysis for malware detection must establish robust monitoring frameworks, deploy advanced security solutions, and train personnel to interpret network anomalies. Network segmentation reduces the attack surface by restricting lateral movement within corporate environments. Enforcing strict access controls, regularly updating firewall rules, and conducting periodic network audits further strengthen defenses against malware infections. By leveraging network traffic analysis alongside endpoint security measures, organizations can enhance their ability to detect, investigate, and respond to malware threats in real time.

Identifying Malware Indicators of Compromise (IoCs)

Indicators of Compromise (IoCs) are critical pieces of forensic evidence used to detect, investigate, and respond to malware infections. These indicators help security teams identify malicious activity within networks and systems, enabling them to mitigate threats before they cause significant damage. IoCs can take various forms, including file hashes, IP addresses, domain names, malicious URLs, registry modifications, process anomalies, and network traffic patterns. By systematically identifying and analyzing IoCs, organizations improve their ability to detect malware infections early and respond effectively to security incidents.

Malware IoCs are typically divided into three main categories: host-based, network-based, and behavioral indicators. Host-based IoCs refer to changes made to a compromised system, such as new or modified files, suspicious processes, registry alterations, and unauthorized system modifications. Network-based IoCs involve indicators related to malicious communication, including C_2 (command-and-control) traffic, DNS anomalies, and unauthorized data exfiltration. Behavioral IoCs focus on identifying patterns in malware execution, such as repeated access to specific system functions, privilege escalation attempts, or evasion techniques.

File hashes are one of the most commonly used IoCs for detecting malware. A hash value is a unique digital fingerprint generated by cryptographic algorithms such as MD5, SHA-1, or SHA-256. Security researchers use hash values to identify and classify malware samples. Once a malware file is discovered, its hash is recorded and shared across threat intelligence platforms. Security tools compare files against known malicious hashes to detect potential infections. However, cybercriminals often modify malware binaries to change their hash values, making hash-based detection less effective against polymorphic threats.

Suspicious file modifications serve as strong host-based IoCs. Malware frequently drops new files, alters existing system files, or injects code into legitimate applications to maintain persistence. Analysts monitor system directories, temporary folders, and startup locations for unexpected file changes. Common malware tactics include renaming executable files to mimic system processes, embedding payloads within legitimate software, and modifying DLL files to hijack execution flow. Security tools track file integrity by comparing current file states with known baselines to detect unauthorized modifications.

Registry changes are another important host-based IoC. Many types of malware, especially trojans and spyware, create or modify registry entries to maintain persistence. Attackers use registry modifications to execute malware at startup, disable security features, or manipulate system behavior. Analysts monitor registry keys such as HKLM\Software\Microsoft\Windows\CurrentVersion\Run for unexpected entries. Malware may also modify registry settings to prevent users from accessing security tools or task managers, ensuring that the infection remains undetected for extended periods.

Suspicious process activity can indicate a malware infection. Analysts monitor running processes for unusual behavior, such as unknown applications consuming excessive system resources, processes launching from uncommon locations, or executables attempting to modify protected files. Malware often injects malicious code into legitimate processes to avoid detection, a technique known as process hollowing. Security teams use tools such as Process Explorer, Task Manager, and Sysmon to track process execution and identify anomalies.

Persistence mechanisms used by malware serve as valuable IoCs. Attackers employ various techniques to ensure that malware remains active even after a system reboot or user intervention. Common persistence methods include scheduled tasks, service modifications, startup folder entries, and browser extensions. Analysts investigate these areas to detect unauthorized configurations that indicate the presence of malware. PowerShell scripts and batch files are also frequently used for persistence, executing commands that automatically restart malware components when a system reboots.

Network-based IoCs provide insights into malware communication and external connections. Malware frequently connects to C2 servers to receive instructions, exfiltrate data, or download additional payloads. Analysts track outbound connections to unknown or suspicious IP addresses, domains, and URLs. Threat intelligence feeds provide lists of known malicious C2 infrastructure, allowing security teams to block malicious traffic at the firewall or intrusion prevention system (IPS) level. Anomalous network traffic patterns, such as repeated DNS lookups to suspicious domains or sudden spikes in data transfer, often indicate malware activity.

Domain Generation Algorithms (DGA) are commonly used by advanced malware strains to evade detection. Instead of using static domain names, malware generates and queries random domain names dynamically. This technique helps attackers avoid domain blacklisting and allows them to switch C2 servers frequently. Analysts detect DGA-based malware by analyzing domain request patterns, identifying unusually structured domain names, and monitoring failed DNS resolutions. Security solutions incorporate machine learning models to detect and block DGA-generated domains in real time.

Encrypted traffic anomalies can signal malware activity. Many modern malware variants use SSL/TLS encryption to hide their communications from security monitoring tools. While encrypted traffic cannot be inspected directly, analysts can identify suspicious behavior by analyzing SSL certificates, handshake patterns, and connection destinations. Self-signed certificates, expired certificate authorities, and repeated connections to untrusted servers often indicate the presence of malware. Deep packet inspection (DPI) and SSL decryption techniques help uncover threats hidden within encrypted network communications.

Anomalous system behaviors serve as strong indicators of malware infections. Security teams look for sudden performance degradation, unexplained disk activity, unusual memory usage, and unauthorized modifications to security settings. Ransomware infections often trigger mass file encryption events, which can be detected by monitoring file system activity. Keyloggers and spyware may generate frequent outbound data transfers, capturing keystrokes or screenshots in real time. Monitoring system logs and event data helps analysts detect these behavioral patterns.

Threat intelligence platforms play a crucial role in IoC identification and sharing. Security researchers contribute IoCs to threat intelligence repositories, allowing organizations to proactively detect and mitigate known threats. Platforms such as VirusTotal, MISP, and AlienVault OTX provide real-time IoC feeds that integrate with security tools. Automated threat intelligence sharing improves industry-wide defenses by enabling organizations to update their security controls with the latest malware signatures, C_2 domains, and attack patterns.

YARA rules enhance IoC-based detection by allowing analysts to define patterns that match known malware characteristics. YARA rules examine file content, API calls, and memory signatures to classify malware variants. Organizations deploy YARA rules in SIEM platforms, endpoint detection and response (EDR) solutions, and network security appliances to detect IoCs dynamically. Heuristic-based YARA rules help identify new threats that exhibit behaviors similar to known malware families, improving proactive threat detection.

Incident response teams use IoCs to track malware infections and contain security breaches. When a compromise is detected, analysts use IoCs to trace the attack chain, identify patient zero, and determine the full scope of the infection. Digital forensics techniques, such as memory analysis and disk imaging, help extract additional IoCs from compromised systems. Security teams update firewall rules, antivirus definitions, and SIEM correlation rules to prevent further exploitation of identified IoCs.

Organizations must continuously update their IoC databases to keep pace with evolving malware threats. Cybercriminals frequently change their tactics, updating C_2 domains, modifying file signatures, and deploying new evasion techniques. By implementing automated IoC enrichment processes, security teams ensure that their defenses remain effective against emerging threats. Machine learning models analyze threat intelligence data, identifying patterns that indicate malware activity before it becomes widespread.

Identifying and analyzing IoCs is a fundamental practice in modern cybersecurity. By correlating host-based, network-based, and behavioral indicators, security teams enhance their ability to detect, investigate, and respond to malware threats. Proactive IoC monitoring strengthens an organization's security posture, reducing the risk of successful cyber attacks and minimizing the impact of malware infections.

Memory Forensics and Volatility Framework

Memory forensics is a critical component of modern cybersecurity investigations, enabling analysts to extract valuable forensic artifacts from volatile system memory. Unlike traditional disk forensics, which focuses on stored files and persistent data, memory forensics examines a system's RAM to identify active processes, hidden malware, encryption keys, network connections, and other transient information. Since many advanced threats operate solely in memory to evade detection, analyzing memory dumps provides security teams with crucial insights into ongoing attacks.

The Volatility Framework is one of the most widely used tools for memory forensics, providing a powerful and flexible platform for extracting and analyzing artifacts from RAM dumps. Developed as an open-source project, Volatility supports a wide range of operating systems, including Windows, Linux, and macOS. It enables security analysts to recover critical information such as running processes, DLLs, network connections, registry keys, and even user credentials stored in memory. By leveraging Volatility, investigators can reconstruct attack timelines, detect malware infections, and gather evidence for incident response.

Memory forensics is particularly useful for detecting fileless malware, which operates entirely in memory without leaving traces on the disk. Attackers use fileless techniques to bypass traditional antivirus and endpoint detection systems. Since these threats execute directly in RAM, they disappear once the system is rebooted, making real-time memory analysis essential for identifying infections. Volatility allows analysts to search for suspicious process injections, API hooks, and memory-resident payloads that indicate the presence of fileless malware.

The process of conducting memory forensics begins with capturing a memory dump from a compromised or suspected system. Several tools, including DumpIt, WinPMEM, FTK Imager, and AVML, facilitate memory acquisition on Windows, Linux, and macOS systems. Once the RAM image is collected, analysts use Volatility to extract forensic data and examine system activity at the time of the snapshot. Since memory snapshots contain volatile data that changes dynamically, acquiring RAM dumps as early as possible during an investigation helps preserve crucial evidence.

One of the most fundamental techniques in memory forensics is process analysis. Volatility provides several plugins that list active processes, terminated processes, and hidden malware masquerading as legitimate applications. The pslist and pstree commands display a hierarchical view of running processes, while psscan identifies processes that were terminated but still exist in memory. By comparing expected system processes with actual memory contents, analysts can detect anomalies such as unauthorized processes, injected code, and suspicious parent-child process relationships.

DLL analysis is another important aspect of memory forensics. Many malware variants inject malicious DLLs into legitimate processes to evade detection. The dlllist command in Volatility retrieves loaded DLLs for each process, helping analysts identify unauthorized modules. Malware often hides by injecting itself into system processes such as explorer.exe or svchost.exe, making DLL enumeration a valuable technique for uncovering hidden threats. The ldrmodules plugin detects injected code in process address spaces, further assisting in malware analysis.

Code injection techniques, such as process hollowing and reflective DLL injection, are commonly used by malware to execute malicious payloads in memory. Process hollowing involves replacing the memory of a legitimate process with malicious code, while reflective DLL injection loads DLLs without using standard Windows API functions.

The malfind plugin in Volatility helps detect injected code by scanning memory for non-standard executable pages. By analyzing injected code sections, security teams can determine the behavior and intent of the malware.

Network forensics is another critical component of memory analysis. Volatility provides plugins such as netscan and connscan to identify active network connections and open sockets at the time of memory capture. Analysts use these plugins to detect unauthorized remote connections, identify C2 servers, and track exfiltrated data. Since many malware variants establish encrypted communication channels, network forensics enables investigators to trace suspicious outbound connections and correlate them with known threat intelligence sources.

Registry analysis in memory forensics helps uncover persistence mechanisms used by malware. Volatility includes plugins like printkey and hivelist that extract Windows registry keys stored in memory. Attackers often modify the registry to achieve persistence by creating autorun entries, disabling security tools, or altering system settings. By analyzing registry artifacts in memory, forensic analysts can identify signs of compromise that may not be evident in disk-based forensics.

Credential harvesting techniques used by malware can also be detected through memory forensics. Attackers frequently use tools such as Mimikatz to extract credentials from LSASS (Local Security Authority Subsystem Service) memory. The dumpcred and lsadump plugins in Volatility retrieve stored credentials, allowing security teams to determine whether an attacker has gained unauthorized access to user accounts. Memory forensics plays a crucial role in identifying credential theft and mitigating lateral movement within a network.

Detecting rootkits through memory forensics is another important use case. Rootkits operate at the kernel level, modifying system structures and hiding malicious processes, files, and registry entries. Volatility includes plugins like modscan and driverscan that help detect hidden kernel modules and unauthorized driver installations. By analyzing kernel memory, security teams can uncover rootkits that evade traditional security tools.

Memory forensic analysis also assists in investigating ransomware attacks. When ransomware encrypts files, it often generates encryption keys and ransom notes in memory before writing them to disk. Analysts use Volatility to extract these artifacts, potentially recovering decryption keys before the system is rebooted. The memdump and procdump plugins allow forensic investigators to retrieve process memory segments for deeper analysis.

Threat hunting operations benefit significantly from memory forensics, as security teams can proactively scan memory dumps for known malware signatures and anomalous behaviors. Volatility integrates with YARA, allowing analysts to apply custom detection rules to memory images. By using YARA rules, forensic teams can automate malware identification, classify threats, and link infections to known adversary groups.

Memory forensics is increasingly valuable in incident response and legal investigations, providing a detailed snapshot of system activity at a specific moment. Unlike disk forensics, which focuses on stored data, memory forensics reveals real-time interactions between processes, users, and network connections. This makes it an essential tool for uncovering advanced threats, detecting insider threats, and reconstructing security breaches.

The evolving complexity of malware necessitates continuous advancements in memory forensics techniques. Security researchers develop new Volatility plugins and forensic methodologies to detect emerging threats. As attackers adopt more sophisticated evasion techniques, such as encrypted memory execution and anti-forensic countermeasures, memory analysis remains a vital component of cybersecurity defense strategies. Organizations that integrate memory forensics into their incident response workflows gain a significant advantage in identifying and mitigating advanced malware threats.

Debugging Malware with OllyDbg and x64dbg

Debugging malware is a crucial technique in reverse engineering, allowing security researchers to analyze malicious code at a granular level. By using debuggers such as OllyDbg and x64dbg, analysts can step through a program's execution, examine registers, inspect memory, and identify the functionality of malicious software. These tools provide a powerful way to analyze packed or obfuscated malware, bypass anti-analysis techniques, and extract useful indicators of compromise (IoCs). Understanding how to use OllyDbg and x64dbg effectively enables security professionals to dissect malware and develop effective countermeasures.

OllyDbg is a 32-bit debugger that operates at the assembly level, providing detailed insights into how a program executes. It is particularly useful for analyzing user-mode Windows malware, such as trojans, keyloggers, and ransomware. OllyDbg allows analysts to set breakpoints, modify register values, and dynamically alter a program's flow to study its behavior. Although OllyDbg is no longer actively maintained, it remains a valuable tool for reversing legacy malware and applications designed for 32-bit Windows environments.

x64dbg is a modern debugger designed for 64-bit applications, making it more suitable for analyzing contemporary malware. It offers a user-friendly interface, advanced scripting capabilities, and extensive plugin support. x64dbg provides similar debugging functionalities as OllyDbg but with additional features tailored for analyzing modern Windows executables. Since many new malware strains target 64-bit architectures, x64dbg has become an essential tool for malware analysts.

The debugging process begins by loading the malware sample into the debugger. Before execution, analysts disable the system's network connection and use an isolated virtual machine (VM) to prevent the malware from causing unintended damage. OllyDbg and x64dbg allow researchers to set breakpoints at key functions, such as CreateProcess, WriteFile, and InternetConnect, to monitor how the malware interacts with the system. By stepping through the code, analysts identify API calls that reveal the malware's purpose and behavior.

Malware often employs packing techniques to obfuscate its code and evade detection. Packers compress or encrypt an executable's original code, decrypting it only during runtime. Debugging packed malware requires analysts to identify the unpacking routine and extract the decrypted code for further analysis. In OllyDbg, analysts search for jmp or call instructions leading to unpacked sections of memory. By setting breakpoints at these instructions and dumping the memory using plugins like OllyDump, analysts recover the original executable for deeper examination. x64dbg provides similar functionality, with its Scylla plugin automating the unpacking process.

String analysis is an important part of debugging malware, as many malicious programs contain hardcoded domains, file paths, or commands. OllyDbg and x64dbg allow analysts to search for ASCII and Unicode strings within an executable's memory space. Strings related to registry modifications, network connections, and encryption keys provide valuable insights into the malware's capabilities. If strings appear obfuscated, analysts track function calls leading to string decryption routines, allowing them to recover hidden text dynamically.

Identifying and bypassing anti-debugging techniques is a common challenge when analyzing malware. Many malicious programs detect the presence of a debugger and alter their behavior to evade analysis. Common anti-debugging techniques include checking for running debuggers with IsDebuggerPresent, modifying the PEB structure, or using timing checks to detect slow execution caused by step-by-step debugging. OllyDbg and x64dbg allow analysts to patch these checks by modifying register values or NOP-ing (No Operation) critical instructions. Plugins such as HideDebugger and TitanHide help bypass anti-debugging mechanisms automatically.

Tracing API calls is another powerful feature of OllyDbg and x64dbg. Malware often relies on Windows API functions to interact with the system, making API tracing essential for understanding its behavior. Analysts set breakpoints on functions like CreateRemoteThread, OpenProcess, and VirtualAlloc to monitor process injection attempts. By analyzing function arguments and return values, researchers determine how the malware manipulates memory, creates new processes, or exfiltrates data. The API Monitor plugin for x64dbg enhances this process by providing real-time function tracing and parameter analysis.

Code injection is a common technique used by malware to evade detection by running within legitimate processes. Debuggers help analysts identify injected code by examining suspicious memory regions and tracing execution flow. Malware often injects itself into processes such as explorer.exe or svchost.exe to blend in with normal system activity. By analyzing the NtCreateThreadEx and WriteProcessMemory API calls, analysts determine how the malware transfers and executes its payload within another process.

Understanding conditional jumps and modifying program flow is crucial in reversing malware behavior. Malware frequently uses conditional jumps (JNZ, JZ, JMP) to execute different code paths based on system conditions. Debuggers allow analysts to manipulate these instructions by modifying flag registers or changing jump conditions. For example, if a malware sample checks for administrative privileges before executing, analysts can alter the condition to force execution, revealing its full functionality.

Extracting embedded payloads and decryption routines is another key aspect of debugging malware. Many malware variants encrypt configuration files, payloads, or communication data to evade detection. Analysts use OllyDbg and x64dbg to locate decryption functions by setting breakpoints on cryptographic APIs such as CryptDecrypt, CryptImportKey, and BCryptDecrypt. By stepping through these functions and extracting decrypted memory contents, researchers obtain valuable threat intelligence, including malware configurations and hardcoded credentials.

Debugging malware also provides insights into persistence mechanisms used to maintain access to infected systems. Malware often modifies the registry, creates scheduled tasks, or installs services to survive reboots. By tracing calls to RegSetValueEx, CreateService, and TaskScheduler functions, analysts determine how the malware ensures persistence. Debuggers allow researchers to identify and remove these modifications, preventing reinfection.

Debugging ransomware is particularly useful in analyzing encryption methods and potential decryption keys. Some ransomware variants store encryption keys in memory before encrypting files. By setting breakpoints on functions such as CryptGenKey and CryptEncrypt, analysts attempt to recover keys before they are deleted. In some cases, debugging has led to the discovery of flaws in ransomware encryption, allowing researchers to develop decryption tools for victims.

Reverse engineering malware with OllyDbg and x64dbg requires patience, expertise, and a structured approach. Analysts must carefully step through execution, document findings, and correlate behavior with known malware techniques. By leveraging debugging tools effectively, security professionals uncover the inner workings of malware, develop better detection mechanisms, and enhance overall cybersecurity defenses. Debugging remains an essential skill in malware analysis, providing deep insights into how malicious programs operate and how they can be neutralized.

Static Analysis with PEStudio and Strings

Static analysis is a fundamental technique in malware research, allowing analysts to examine executable files without executing them. By inspecting file structures, embedded resources, and metadata, analysts gain valuable insights into a malware sample's functionality, potential threats, and detection evasion techniques. Tools like PEStudio and Strings are widely used in static malware analysis, helping researchers identify malicious indicators, suspicious API calls, embedded configurations, and hardcoded domains. Unlike dynamic analysis, which involves running malware in a controlled environment, static analysis provides an initial layer of investigation that helps determine whether further analysis is necessary.

PEStudio is a powerful static analysis tool designed to analyze Windows Portable Executable (PE) files, including .exe, .dll, and .sys files. It extracts a wide range of information from PE headers, imported libraries, function calls, and embedded resources. By examining these components, analysts can determine whether an executable contains suspicious behavior, indicators of compromise (IoCs), or obfuscation techniques. PEStudio also integrates with external reputation services, providing insights into whether a file has been flagged as malicious by the cybersecurity community.

One of the first steps in using PEStudio is analyzing the PE header, which contains metadata about the executable. The PE header includes details such as the compilation timestamp, target architecture (32-bit or 64-bit), and section table information. Malware authors often manipulate timestamps to disguise the true origin of a file, making it harder to attribute attacks. Analysts compare compilation dates with known threat reports to identify anomalies. Additionally, checking the PE checksum and signature verification helps determine whether the file has been tampered with.

The imported functions section of a PE file provides critical insights into its capabilities. When an executable runs, it relies on system libraries (DLLs) to perform various operations such as file handling, network communication, and process creation. PEStudio extracts imported functions and highlights those associated with suspicious activities. For example, functions like CreateRemoteThread, WriteProcessMemory, and VirtualAllocEx are commonly used in process injection attacks. Network-related APIs such as InternetOpenUrl, WinHttpConnect, and send indicate potential command-and-control (C2) communications. Analysts focus on these imports to assess whether the file exhibits malware-like behavior.

Another important aspect of PEStudio analysis is detecting packed or obfuscated executables. Many malware authors use packers and crypters to hide malicious code from antivirus software. A packed binary often has few or no imported functions because the real code is decrypted dynamically during execution. PEStudio flags such anomalies by analyzing entropy levels and identifying suspicious section names such as .text, .rsrc, or .upx. High entropy in a section suggests that the data may be compressed or encrypted, indicating potential obfuscation techniques used to evade detection.

PEStudio also extracts embedded resources, including icons, images, configuration files, and hidden scripts. Malware often stores its payloads within the resource section of an executable to avoid detection. Analysts inspect these resources to identify embedded shellcode, phishing web pages, or fake error messages used in social engineering attacks. Extracting and analyzing these components helps researchers understand the full functionality of a malware sample without executing it.

In addition to PEStudio, the Strings tool is widely used in static analysis to extract readable text from binary files. Many malware samples contain hardcoded strings that reveal important details about their operations, including C2 server addresses, encryption keys, user-agent strings, and error messages. The Strings tool scans an executable's memory and file contents for ASCII and Unicode text, providing a quick way to uncover hidden information.

Analysts often use Strings to search for specific keywords related to malware behavior. For example, if a malware sample contains references to cmd.exe, powershell.exe, or rundll32.exe, it likely executes system commands or loads additional payloads. Strings related to registry modifications, such as HKLM\Software\Microsoft\Windows\CurrentVersion\Run, indicate that the malware may establish persistence by modifying startup settings. Searching for phrases like HTTP, GET, or POST helps identify network activity and potential C2 communication endpoints.

Malware developers sometimes attempt to evade static analysis by obfuscating strings or storing them in encoded formats. Common obfuscation techniques include Base64 encoding, XOR encryption, and hexadecimal encoding. To uncover these hidden strings, analysts use additional tools such as CyberChef, Base64 decoders, and scripting languages like Python to decode and analyze suspicious text. Identifying and reversing string obfuscation techniques is crucial for extracting meaningful IoCs from malware samples.

Comparing extracted strings against known malware databases enhances threat intelligence efforts. Analysts cross-reference suspicious strings with public malware repositories, sandbox reports, and threat intelligence feeds to determine whether a sample matches previously identified threats. If a malware sample contains known campaign identifiers, analysts can attribute it to a specific threat actor or malware family, aiding in attribution and response efforts.

Static analysis with PEStudio and Strings also helps detect ransomware, banking trojans, and spyware variants. Ransomware often contains strings related to encryption keys, ransom notes, and payment instructions. Banking trojans include references to financial institutions, fake login pages, and credential theft functions. Spyware samples may contain keywords related to keystroke logging, screen capturing, or webcam access. By analyzing extracted strings, researchers classify malware types and determine their objectives.

Threat hunting operations benefit significantly from static analysis, as it allows analysts to filter and prioritize suspicious files before executing them in a controlled environment. Organizations use automated malware triage systems that integrate PEStudio and Strings to classify incoming threats efficiently. By applying YARA rules to extracted strings, security teams automate the detection of malware families based on predefined patterns.

While static analysis alone cannot reveal all aspects of a malware sample, it provides an essential starting point for deeper investigations. Combining PEStudio and Strings with dynamic analysis techniques, such as sandboxing and debugging, enhances overall malware detection capabilities. Analysts use static indicators to develop targeted execution strategies, focusing on areas of interest revealed during the initial analysis phase.

Cybercriminals continuously evolve their evasion techniques to bypass static analysis, using sophisticated encryption, anti-analysis mechanisms, and polymorphic code to generate unique signatures. However, static analysis remains a valuable tool in the malware analyst's arsenal, providing rapid insights into potential threats before engaging in more complex reverse engineering. Security professionals rely on tools like PEStudio and Strings to accelerate malware classification, identify IoCs, and enhance threat intelligence sharing across the cybersecurity community.

Dynamic Analysis with Cuckoo Sandbox

Dynamic analysis is a fundamental technique for understanding how malware behaves when executed in a controlled environment. One of the most widely used tools for this purpose is Cuckoo Sandbox, an open-source automated malware analysis system that provides detailed insights into a file's runtime behavior. Unlike static analysis, which examines a file's structure without executing it, dynamic analysis with Cuckoo Sandbox allows security professionals to observe system modifications, network activity, and process interactions in real time. By executing malware samples in an isolated virtual machine, analysts can safely monitor their behavior and extract valuable indicators of compromise (IoCs).

Cuckoo Sandbox operates by setting up a virtualized environment where malware can execute without affecting the host system. It supports multiple operating systems, including Windows, Linux, and macOS, making it highly versatile for analyzing different types of threats. The sandbox records all interactions between the malware and the operating system, capturing file modifications, registry changes, API calls, network connections, and process activity. This level of detail enables researchers to classify malware, detect evasive techniques, and understand its intended functionality.

Setting up Cuckoo Sandbox involves configuring a host system to manage and analyze malware within a virtualized guest machine. The host machine runs the Cuckoo analysis framework, while the guest machine acts as the execution environment. The guest machine is configured with monitoring tools, such as Sysinternals Process Monitor, Wireshark for network traffic capture, and API hooking mechanisms to track system calls. By maintaining a clean snapshot of the guest machine, analysts can reset it after each analysis to ensure a fresh environment for the next sample.

Once a malware sample is submitted to Cuckoo, the sandbox begins execution and records every action performed by the file. Analysts review the generated reports, which provide a breakdown of system modifications, file creations, registry alterations, and network communications. Cuckoo also generates process trees that illustrate how malware spawns child processes, injects code into legitimate applications, or escalates privileges. These insights help security teams determine the malware's impact and its methods of persistence.

A key feature of Cuckoo Sandbox is its ability to capture and analyze network traffic. Malware frequently communicates with command-and-control (C2) servers to receive instructions, exfiltrate data, or download additional payloads. Cuckoo logs all outbound connections, DNS requests, and HTTP interactions made by the malware during execution. Analysts inspect these network traces to identify suspicious IP addresses, domain names, and encryption patterns. If malware uses domain generation algorithms (DGA) to evade detection, Cuckoo records the generated domains, allowing security teams to block them proactively.

Malware often employs process injection techniques to hide its presence and execute within legitimate applications. Cuckoo Sandbox detects process hollowing, DLL injection, and thread hijacking by monitoring memory modifications and API calls. Attackers use these techniques to evade signature-based antivirus detection, making behavioral analysis in a sandbox essential for identifying stealthy threats. By tracking process creation and injected code segments, analysts can uncover hidden malware functionality and extract executable payloads for further analysis.

Persistence mechanisms are another critical aspect of malware behavior. Many threats attempt to establish persistence by modifying startup configurations, creating scheduled tasks, or altering system services. Cuckoo Sandbox logs registry modifications, autorun entries, and service installations, helping analysts detect how malware survives system reboots. Identifying these persistence methods is essential for developing effective removal strategies and preventing reinfection.

Cuckoo also provides behavioral signatures that help classify malware families based on their runtime actions. By comparing observed behaviors against known patterns, Cuckoo automatically identifies threats such as ransomware, banking trojans, or information stealers.

Behavioral signatures detect specific techniques used by different malware families, such as keylogging, credential theft, or disk encryption. These automated classifications assist security teams in rapidly assessing the severity and impact of a malware sample.

Advanced malware often incorporates anti-analysis techniques to evade detection in sandbox environments. Some malware samples detect whether they are running in a virtual machine and modify their behavior accordingly. Common sandbox detection methods include checking system uptime, querying hardware properties, and searching for virtualization artifacts. Cuckoo includes features to counteract these evasion techniques by simulating real user activity, randomizing machine identifiers, and modifying system configurations to appear more like a physical environment.

Ransomware analysis benefits greatly from sandboxing with Cuckoo. Since ransomware encrypts files upon execution, running it in a controlled environment allows analysts to observe its encryption routines, identify targeted file extensions, and detect dropped ransom notes. By extracting decryption keys or identifying flaws in encryption implementations, researchers can develop decryptors to help victims recover their files. Cuckoo captures every stage of ransomware execution, from initial infection to final payload execution.

Malware variants that target specific industries or geographic regions can be analyzed in Cuckoo by simulating different environments. Some malware samples remain dormant unless they detect a particular system language, keyboard layout, or IP range. Analysts configure Cuckoo to mimic targeted environments by modifying system settings, installing region-specific software, and adjusting localization parameters. These techniques help uncover threats that otherwise remain undetected in standard sandbox configurations.

Threat intelligence integration enhances the capabilities of Cuckoo Sandbox by correlating analysis results with external security databases. Cuckoo connects with threat intelligence platforms such as VirusTotal, Hybrid Analysis, and MISP to compare analyzed samples against known malware signatures. This integration helps security teams determine whether a sample is part of an ongoing attack campaign or linked to previously identified threats. By sharing IoCs extracted from Cuckoo reports, organizations improve collective defense efforts against cyber threats.

Incident response teams rely on Cuckoo Sandbox to quickly triage and investigate potential malware infections. When a suspicious email attachment or executable is detected, analysts submit it to Cuckoo for immediate analysis. The sandbox generates a comprehensive report detailing the malware's behavior, allowing responders to assess the risk level and take appropriate actions. By automating malware analysis, Cuckoo reduces response times and enables security teams to contain threats more effectively.

Organizations deploy Cuckoo Sandbox as part of a layered security approach, integrating it with SIEM (Security Information and Event Management) systems and endpoint protection solutions. By continuously analyzing incoming files and attachments, Cuckoo helps detect emerging threats before they infiltrate corporate networks. Automated malware sandboxing enhances threat detection capabilities and strengthens cybersecurity defenses against advanced persistent threats (APTs) and zero-day exploits.

As malware becomes more sophisticated, dynamic analysis with Cuckoo Sandbox remains a critical tool for security professionals. Its ability to execute and monitor malware in a controlled environment provides deep insights into malicious behaviors, attack techniques, and network indicators. By leveraging Cuckoo for malware research, security teams improve detection accuracy, enhance incident response capabilities, and develop more effective defense strategies against evolving cyber threats.

Writing Custom Tools for Malware Analysis

Malware analysis is a constantly evolving field that requires analysts to adapt their techniques and tools to keep up with emerging threats. While there are many powerful commercial and open-source tools available for analyzing malware, certain cases require customized solutions tailored to specific analysis needs. Writing custom tools for malware analysis provides greater flexibility, automation, and deeper insights into how malicious code operates. Security researchers develop their own scripts and utilities to extract indicators of compromise (IoCs), automate repetitive tasks, and analyze malware in unique ways that commercial tools may not support.

Developing custom malware analysis tools typically involves scripting languages such as Python, PowerShell, and Bash, as well as low-level programming languages like C and C++ for more advanced functionality. Python is particularly popular among malware analysts due to its simplicity, extensive libraries, and ability to automate tasks such as parsing binary files, extracting metadata, and analyzing network traffic. Frameworks such as pefile, pyshark, Scapy, and YARA allow researchers to write powerful analysis scripts with minimal effort.

One of the most common uses of custom tools is automating static analysis. Analysts often need to extract information from Portable Executable (PE) files, such as imported libraries, section headers, and embedded resources. Writing a Python script using the pefile library enables analysts to quickly parse PE headers and identify suspicious attributes. A simple script can extract the entry point, timestamp, digital signatures, and API imports, helping to determine whether an executable contains malicious behavior. Automating these checks reduces the time spent manually inspecting each sample and improves overall efficiency.

Another valuable application of custom tools is analyzing embedded strings within malware binaries. While tools like Strings and BinText provide basic string extraction, a custom script can improve results by filtering out irrelevant data, decoding obfuscated strings, and applying regex patterns to highlight important information. Malware often stores C2 domains, file paths, and encryption keys as encoded or compressed data. Writing a custom script that applies Base64 decoding, XOR decryption, or reverse string reconstruction helps analysts uncover hidden information that standard tools might overlook.

Custom tools also play a key role in network traffic analysis for malware detection. Many malware samples communicate with external servers to receive commands, exfiltrate data, or download additional payloads. Writing a Python script using Scapy or pyshark allows analysts to filter packets, extract suspicious domains, and detect anomalies in network traffic. A script can be designed to monitor DNS requests for unusual patterns, identify encrypted communication channels, or compare traffic against known threat intelligence feeds. By automating these checks, analysts can rapidly detect and block malicious network activity.

Memory forensics is another area where custom tools enhance malware analysis. While tools like Volatility provide extensive functionality, writing custom Volatility plugins allows researchers to extract specific artifacts related to a particular malware family. A custom plugin can focus on identifying injected code, extracting decryption keys from memory, or detecting unusual process behaviors. By tailoring memory analysis tools to specific threats, analysts gain deeper insights into how malware operates and evades detection.

Automating dynamic analysis is another advantage of writing custom tools. Many malware analysis tasks involve running a sample in a controlled environment and monitoring its behavior. While tools like Cuckoo Sandbox provide automated analysis, custom scripts can extend their functionality by collecting additional data, triggering specific execution paths, or interacting with the malware dynamically. For example, a script can simulate user input, modify registry settings, or alter system time to test how malware responds to different conditions. These custom interactions help uncover hidden functionality that might not be triggered under normal execution.

Reverse engineering malware often requires decoding obfuscated payloads and unpacking encrypted binaries. Writing custom unpackers allows analysts to automate the extraction of hidden code sections. Many malware families use packers to compress or encrypt their payloads, making them difficult to analyze statically. By writing a script that hooks decryption routines, dumps memory at specific execution points, or reconstructs the original binary, analysts can bypass obfuscation and retrieve the raw malware code for further investigation.

Developing custom tools also helps in detecting malware persistence mechanisms. Many threats modify the Windows registry, create scheduled tasks, or install services to ensure they execute upon reboot. A script that scans the system for new registry keys, monitors startup folders, and lists scheduled tasks allows analysts to identify unauthorized modifications. Automating these checks makes it easier to track changes over time and detect malware persistence techniques that might otherwise go unnoticed.

Custom tools can also be used for YARA rule generation and signature-based detection. YARA is a powerful tool for classifying and detecting malware based on byte patterns and strings. Writing a script that automatically extracts relevant byte sequences from malware samples and generates YARA rules streamlines the process of threat detection. Analysts can also develop tools that apply machine learning techniques to cluster malware samples based on shared characteristics, improving the efficiency of detection and classification efforts.

Building tools for analyzing logs and forensic artifacts further enhances malware research. Many organizations collect system logs, endpoint telemetry, and event traces from infected machines. Writing a script that correlates logs, extracts timestamps, and visualizes attack timelines helps analysts reconstruct security incidents. Custom log analysis tools provide a structured approach to investigating malware infections and identifying patterns of compromise across multiple systems.

Sharing and collaborating on custom malware analysis tools benefits the cybersecurity community as a whole. Many researchers contribute open-source tools to repositories like GitHub, allowing others to use, modify, and improve them. Security professionals create and maintain custom toolkits for specific malware families, providing ready-to-use solutions for detecting and analyzing emerging threats. Contributing to open-source projects fosters innovation and accelerates the development of advanced malware analysis techniques.

Writing custom tools for malware analysis not only enhances an analyst's capabilities but also allows for greater adaptability in responding to evolving cyber threats. Off-the-shelf security tools have limitations, and customizing scripts to address specific challenges enables deeper insights into malware behavior. Security researchers who develop their own tools gain a deeper understanding of malware techniques, automate repetitive tasks, and contribute to the broader cybersecurity ecosystem. By continuously improving and refining these tools, analysts can stay ahead of cybercriminals and enhance their ability to detect and mitigate malware infections.

Automating Malware Analysis with Python

Malware analysis is a time-consuming and complex process that requires analysts to examine malicious files, extract indicators of compromise (IoCs), and determine the impact of an infection. Automation plays a crucial role in improving efficiency and accuracy in malware analysis, and Python has become the preferred programming language for automating these tasks. With its rich ecosystem of libraries, Python enables analysts to develop custom tools that streamline static and dynamic analysis, automate network forensics, and enhance detection capabilities. By automating repetitive tasks, security teams can process large volumes of malware samples efficiently while focusing on more advanced investigations.

Python's simplicity and extensive libraries make it ideal for automating static analysis, which involves extracting useful information from malware samples without executing them. The pefile library allows analysts to parse Portable Executable (PE) headers, providing details about the malware's structure, imports, and sections. A Python script using pefile can automatically extract critical attributes such as the entry point, timestamp, imported functions, and digital signatures. This automation helps analysts quickly determine whether a file exhibits suspicious characteristics before conducting more in-depth analysis.

Extracting embedded strings from malware samples is another common task that can be automated with Python. The strings module or direct binary parsing can be used to retrieve readable ASCII and Unicode text from executable files. Malware often contains hardcoded URLs, IP addresses, registry keys, and command-and-control (C2) domains. Writing a Python script to filter out meaningless strings and highlight relevant keywords significantly reduces the time spent manually searching for valuable information. Additionally, Python's base64 and binascii modules help decode encoded strings, revealing hidden malware configurations and embedded payloads.

Python is also widely used in automating YARA-based malware classification. YARA is a rule-based engine for identifying malware by matching patterns within files. By integrating YARA with Python, analysts can automatically scan directories, analyze multiple samples, and generate reports based on detected signatures. The yara-python library allows analysts to create and execute YARA rules within scripts, enabling real-time detection and classification of malware families. This approach is especially useful for security teams handling large-scale malware collections, as it allows for rapid triage and threat categorization.

Dynamic analysis, which involves executing malware in a controlled environment, can also be automated using Python. The subprocess module allows analysts to automate the execution of samples within a virtual machine or sandbox environment. Python scripts can launch a malware sample, monitor system activity, and capture logs without requiring manual intervention. Integration with sandboxing platforms such as Cuckoo Sandbox enables Python scripts to submit files for execution, retrieve analysis reports, and extract key behavioral indicators. By automating these processes, security teams gain real-time visibility into malware behavior while reducing the risk of accidental infections.

Python is particularly useful for automating network traffic analysis, a crucial aspect of detecting malware communications. The Scapy library allows analysts to capture, filter, and analyze packets to detect unusual network activity. A Python script using Scapy can monitor DNS requests, extract HTTP headers, and detect suspicious connections to known malicious IP addresses. Automating network forensics helps analysts identify command-and-control infrastructure, track data exfiltration, and detect malware attempting to evade detection through encrypted tunnels or domain generation algorithms (DGA).

Python can also be used to automate API interaction with threat intelligence services. Platforms such as VirusTotal, Hybrid Analysis, and MISP provide APIs that allow analysts to query file hashes, domains, and URLs for known threat intelligence. Writing a Python script using the requests library enables automated lookups, retrieving reputation scores and analysis results without manual searching. This automation helps analysts correlate malware samples with existing threat intelligence, improving detection accuracy and response times.

Memory forensics is another area where Python automation enhances malware analysis. The Volatility Framework, a powerful tool for analyzing memory dumps, provides a Python API for extracting forensic artifacts. By scripting Volatility commands, analysts can automate the retrieval of running processes, injected code, open network connections, and credentials stored in memory. Python scripts can also be used to scan memory dumps for specific patterns, detect rootkits, and identify hidden processes that traditional endpoint security solutions may miss.

Malware analysts often need to unpack and decrypt obfuscated malware payloads, a task that can be automated using Python. Many malware samples use custom packers to evade detection, requiring analysts to extract the original payload for further analysis. Python scripts can hook decryption routines, simulate unpacking sequences, and reconstruct the original executable. The uncompyle6 library helps decompile Python-based malware, while pycrypto and cryptography modules allow analysts to reverse-engineer encryption algorithms used by malware to protect its payloads.

Python automation extends to malware sandboxing, where security teams create isolated environments to safely analyze threats. By using Python scripts to manage virtual machines, execute malware, and collect logs, analysts can standardize their analysis workflow. The pyvmomi library allows for the automation of VMware environments, while vboxapi provides similar capabilities for VirtualBox. Automating malware execution and behavior tracking within sandboxes improves efficiency and ensures repeatable testing conditions.

Incident response teams benefit from Python automation by developing custom scripts that detect and remediate infections across multiple endpoints. Python scripts can be deployed via remote execution frameworks such as paramiko for SSH access or winrm for Windows environments. These scripts scan for IoCs, remove malware artifacts, and restore system configurations automatically. By integrating Python automation with Security Information and Event Management (SIEM) solutions, security teams can respond to threats in real time and reduce the impact of malware infections.

Python also facilitates malware behavior correlation and clustering. By analyzing similarities in API calls, imported functions, and file structures, Python scripts can group malware samples into families. Machine learning models built with scikit-learn or tensorflow further enhance malware classification by detecting patterns across thousands of samples. Automating this process allows researchers to identify new malware variants and track evolving attack campaigns with greater accuracy.

Sharing Python automation scripts with the security community enhances collective defense efforts. Many cybersecurity professionals contribute tools and frameworks to open-source repositories such as GitHub, allowing others to improve and extend them. Python-based projects such as Flare-Floss for deobfuscation, CAPE for automated malware analysis, and Viper for malware collection demonstrate the power of automation in malware research. By collaborating and refining automated analysis techniques, security teams strengthen their ability to detect and mitigate threats.

Python's versatility and extensive library support make it an essential tool for automating malware analysis. By scripting repetitive tasks, enhancing detection capabilities, and integrating with existing security frameworks, Python enables analysts to efficiently process malware samples, uncover hidden threats, and respond to cyberattacks faster. The continuous development of Python-based automation tools ensures that security professionals stay ahead of evolving malware techniques, improving their ability to protect systems from malicious threats.

Legal and Ethical Considerations in Malware Analysis

Malware analysis is a crucial aspect of cybersecurity, providing security professionals with insights into how malicious software operates and how to defend against it. However, conducting malware analysis involves significant legal and ethical considerations that analysts must be aware of to avoid violating laws, infringing on privacy, or unintentionally causing harm. Understanding these considerations ensures that malware research is conducted responsibly, legally, and ethically, protecting both analysts and the organizations they work for.

One of the most fundamental legal concerns in malware analysis is compliance with computer crime laws. Many countries have strict regulations regarding the possession, distribution, and execution of malicious code. Laws such as the U.S. Computer Fraud and Abuse Act (CFAA), the UK Computer Misuse Act, and the European Union's General Data Protection Regulation (GDPR) impose limitations on unauthorized access, data collection, and malware handling. Analysts must ensure that their work does not inadvertently violate these laws by obtaining proper authorization before analyzing malware or accessing compromised systems.

Handling malware samples responsibly is another critical legal consideration. Malware often contains stolen data, proprietary code, or personally identifiable information (PII) from victims. Extracting, storing, or sharing such data without proper authorization can lead to legal consequences, including violations of privacy laws. Security professionals should implement strict controls when handling malware samples, ensuring that no unauthorized data is accessed, stored, or distributed. Secure storage practices, encryption, and controlled access to malware repositories help prevent misuse and accidental exposure.

Another ethical concern in malware analysis is the risk of unintentional harm. Malware research must be conducted in isolated environments, such as sandboxes or air-gapped networks, to prevent accidental infections that could impact production systems or external networks. Analysts must take precautions to ensure that malware samples do not escape controlled environments, as unintentional leaks can lead to widespread infections or security incidents. Strict containment measures, such as virtual machines with restricted network access and strict firewall rules, help mitigate these risks.

Sharing malware analysis results with the cybersecurity community is a common practice that contributes to collective defense. However, researchers must be cautious about how they disclose findings, ensuring that sensitive details are not leaked to adversaries. Responsible disclosure involves coordinating with affected organizations, software vendors, and law enforcement agencies before publicly releasing information about vulnerabilities or exploits. If a researcher discovers a zero-day vulnerability while analyzing malware, responsible disclosure ensures that patches can be developed before attackers exploit the flaw further.

Reverse engineering malware presents additional legal and ethical challenges. In some jurisdictions, reverse engineering is restricted under software licensing agreements or intellectual property laws. Malware analysts must understand the legal boundaries of reverse engineering, particularly when analyzing proprietary software that has been repurposed for malicious activities. Organizations should establish clear policies on reverse engineering practices to ensure compliance with applicable laws and regulations.

Collaboration with law enforcement and government agencies introduces further ethical considerations. While malware analysts often work with these entities to track cybercriminal activities, they must also consider issues related to privacy, surveillance, and due process. Security professionals must balance the need for cyber threat intelligence sharing with respect for individuals' rights and ethical standards. Transparency in how data is collected, shared, and used is essential for maintaining public trust and ethical integrity in cybersecurity research.

Another controversial aspect of malware research involves offensive security and active defense measures. Some organizations engage in "hack back" operations, where they attempt to retaliate against cyber attackers by infiltrating their infrastructure or disabling malicious servers. While this approach may seem justified from a defensive perspective, it raises significant legal and ethical issues, including potential violations of international laws and unintended collateral damage. Engaging in offensive cyber activities without legal authorization can lead to severe consequences, including criminal charges.

Ethical considerations also extend to the use of artificial intelligence (AI) and automation in malware analysis. As AI-powered malware detection tools become more advanced, questions arise about bias in detection algorithms, potential false positives, and accountability for automated security decisions. Analysts must ensure that AI-driven malware classification systems are transparent, fair, and free from biases that could lead to unintended security incidents or wrongful attributions. Ethical AI practices in cybersecurity help maintain trust in automated threat detection and response mechanisms.

The use of honeypots and deception techniques in malware analysis presents additional ethical dilemmas. While honeypots are valuable tools for studying attacker behavior and collecting threat intelligence, they must be deployed responsibly to avoid legal repercussions. Security teams should ensure that honeypots do not entrap innocent users or violate privacy regulations. Additionally, the data collected from honeypots must be handled securely to prevent unauthorized access or misuse.

Security researchers conducting malware analysis must also consider the ethical implications of publishing exploit details. While publicizing malware techniques can help defenders understand threats, it can also provide attackers with additional knowledge to refine their tactics. Researchers should carefully evaluate the potential risks and benefits of publishing detailed malware analyses, ensuring that security improvements outweigh the risks of empowering malicious actors. In some cases, redacted or limited-disclosure reports strike a balance between information sharing and responsible security practices.

Educational and training initiatives in malware analysis must adhere to ethical guidelines to prevent misuse. Universities and cybersecurity training programs must ensure that students are taught responsible malware handling practices and that their research is conducted under strict supervision. Providing access to malware samples without proper controls can lead to unintended consequences, such as the spread of malware or unauthorized experimentation. Establishing ethical guidelines for training programs helps prevent the misuse of malware analysis skills.

Companies conducting malware research must implement clear policies on ethical guidelines, ensuring that employees understand their legal obligations and responsibilities. Establishing a code of conduct for malware analysts helps maintain professionalism, integrity, and compliance with regulatory standards. Organizations should provide ongoing training on legal and ethical considerations, helping security teams navigate complex issues related to malware research, privacy, and cybersecurity ethics.

The evolving nature of cyber threats requires constant adaptation in legal and ethical considerations. As new attack techniques emerge, laws and ethical guidelines must evolve to address challenges such as ransomware investigations, state-sponsored cyber operations, and global cybercrime enforcement. Collaboration between the cybersecurity industry, policymakers, and legal experts is essential for developing frameworks that balance security needs with ethical responsibility.

Legal and ethical considerations in malware analysis play a crucial role in ensuring that cybersecurity research is conducted responsibly. Security professionals must be aware of the legal frameworks governing malware research, follow ethical guidelines in handling malware samples, and take precautions to prevent unintended harm. By adhering to best practices, analysts contribute to a safer digital environment while maintaining trust, transparency, and accountability in cybersecurity investigations.

Responding to Malware Incidents

Malware incidents can have devastating consequences for organizations, ranging from data breaches and financial losses to system downtime and reputational damage. A structured and efficient response to malware incidents is crucial for minimizing the impact of an infection and restoring normal operations. Incident response involves a series of coordinated steps designed to detect, contain, analyze, and remediate the effects of malware while ensuring that future incidents can be prevented or mitigated. A well-prepared malware response strategy enables security teams to act quickly, reducing the likelihood of widespread damage and data loss.

The first step in responding to a malware incident is detection and identification. Malware can enter an organization's network through phishing emails, malicious attachments, drive-by downloads, or exploited vulnerabilities. Security teams rely on endpoint detection and response (EDR) solutions, antivirus software, intrusion detection systems (IDS), and security information and event management (SIEM) platforms to identify potential malware infections. Employees may also report suspicious system behavior, such as slow performance, unexpected pop-ups, unauthorized file changes, or disabled security controls. Once malware activity is detected, it is essential to verify the infection by analyzing affected files, monitoring network traffic, and reviewing system logs.

Containment is the next critical phase of malware incident response. The goal of containment is to prevent the malware from spreading further within the network and causing additional damage. Security teams isolate infected machines by disconnecting them from the network, disabling remote access, and restricting compromised accounts. Network segmentation and firewall rules help limit the spread of malware by blocking communication with command-and-control (C2) servers. In cases where malware is actively encrypting files or exfiltrating data, immediate containment actions can minimize the impact of the attack.

After containment, security teams proceed with malware analysis to determine the nature of the infection and its potential risks. Static and dynamic analysis techniques help analysts understand the malware's behavior, persistence mechanisms, and communication channels. Using tools such as PEStudio, YARA, and Cuckoo Sandbox, researchers examine the malware sample's executable structure, API calls, and network activity. If the malware has been observed before, threat intelligence feeds and databases such as VirusTotal and MITRE ATT&CK can provide valuable context about its origins and known countermeasures. For new or sophisticated threats, reverse engineering may be required to uncover hidden capabilities and identify appropriate remediation steps.

Once the malware's behavior is understood, the eradication phase begins. Security teams remove malicious files, terminate infected processes, and eliminate registry modifications or scheduled tasks created by the malware. Automated scripts and security tools are used to scan for and remove malware artifacts across affected systems. If the malware has established persistence, analysts must identify and neutralize all persistence mechanisms to prevent reinfection. Removing unauthorized accounts, resetting credentials, and updating security configurations are essential steps in this phase. If a system has been severely compromised, a full reinstallation of the operating system may be necessary to ensure complete eradication.

Recovery focuses on restoring affected systems and verifying that normal operations can resume without further risk. Backups play a crucial role in this phase, as organizations rely on clean, up-to-date backups to restore lost or encrypted data. Before restoring systems from backups, security teams ensure that backup files are free of malware to prevent reintroducing the infection. Logging and monitoring tools help detect any lingering threats that may have been missed during eradication. Updating software, patching vulnerabilities, and applying security updates further reduce the risk of another infection.

Once recovery is complete, organizations conduct a post-incident analysis to assess what went wrong and how similar incidents can be prevented in the future. Incident response teams review logs, analyze attack patterns, and evaluate response effectiveness to identify gaps in security controls. A detailed incident report documents the timeline of the attack, the malware's behavior, response actions taken, and recommendations for improving security posture. Organizations use this information to refine their incident response plans, enhance security awareness training, and implement stronger defensive measures.

Communication during a malware incident is also critical. Security teams coordinate with IT administrators, executives, legal teams, and external stakeholders to ensure that the incident is handled appropriately. If sensitive data has been compromised, organizations may be required to notify affected parties, regulatory bodies, or law enforcement agencies. Transparency in reporting incidents helps build trust and demonstrates a commitment to cybersecurity best practices.

Proactive threat hunting and continuous monitoring help organizations detect and respond to malware threats before they escalate into major incidents. Security teams analyze historical logs, endpoint activities, and network traffic for signs of compromise. Threat intelligence integration enhances detection capabilities by correlating new threats with previously identified attack patterns. Regular security assessments, penetration testing, and red team exercises further strengthen an organization's ability to detect and respond to malware infections effectively.

User education and awareness training are essential components of malware prevention and incident response. Employees should be trained to recognize phishing attempts, avoid suspicious downloads, and report anomalies in system behavior. Simulated phishing campaigns and security awareness programs help reinforce best practices and reduce the likelihood of malware infections caused by human error. Organizations that invest in cybersecurity training empower their workforce to act as the first line of defense against malware threats.

Automation plays a key role in improving incident response efficiency. Security orchestration, automation, and response (SOAR) platforms integrate with existing security tools to automate threat detection, containment, and remediation processes. Automated malware analysis, real-time threat intelligence correlation, and behavioral anomaly detection enable security teams to respond to malware incidents faster and more effectively. By reducing manual effort, automation allows analysts to focus on investigating complex threats and improving response strategies.

Malware incident response is an ongoing process that requires organizations to continuously adapt to new threats. Cybercriminals constantly develop more advanced techniques, including fileless malware, polymorphic threats, and ransomware variants designed to evade traditional security measures. Organizations must stay ahead by regularly updating their security tools, refining response procedures, and collaborating with industry peers to share threat intelligence. By maintaining a strong security posture and implementing a well-defined malware response plan, organizations can minimize the impact of infections and enhance their resilience against evolving cyber threats.

Case Studies of Major Malware Attacks

Throughout history, malware attacks have had devastating consequences for organizations, governments, and individuals. By examining major malware incidents, security professionals gain insights into attack methodologies, vulnerabilities exploited, and the impact of cyber threats. Understanding these cases helps organizations strengthen defenses and improve incident response strategies. Some of the most significant malware attacks in history have highlighted weaknesses in cybersecurity and the evolving tactics of cybercriminals.

One of the most infamous malware attacks was WannaCry, a global ransomware outbreak that occurred in May 2017. WannaCry exploited a vulnerability in Microsoft Windows known as EternalBlue, which was leaked by the Shadow Brokers, a hacking group that allegedly obtained cyber weapons developed by the U.S. National Security Agency (NSA). Using this exploit, WannaCry spread rapidly across networks without requiring user interaction, encrypting files on infected machines and demanding a Bitcoin ransom for decryption. The attack affected over 200,000 computers in 150 countries, crippling hospitals, government agencies, and businesses. The attack was eventually halted when a security researcher discovered a kill switch domain that, when registered, stopped the ransomware's spread. WannaCry underscored the importance of timely software updates and the dangers of using outdated operating systems.

Another significant malware attack was NotPetya, a destructive wiper disguised as ransomware that struck in June 2017. Originally targeting Ukrainian organizations, NotPetya spread globally, causing billions of dollars in damages. The malware used the same EternalBlue exploit as WannaCry but was far more destructive. Unlike traditional ransomware, NotPetya irreversibly encrypted system files without providing a functional decryption key, effectively rendering infected systems useless. Major corporations, including Maersk, FedEx, and Merck, suffered substantial financial losses due to widespread disruptions. NotPetya is widely believed to have been a state-sponsored cyberattack linked to Russian hackers, demonstrating how malware can be used as a weapon in cyber warfare.

The Stuxnet attack remains one of the most sophisticated malware operations ever discovered. First identified in 2010, Stuxnet was designed to sabotage Iran's nuclear program by targeting industrial control systems (ICS). Unlike conventional malware, Stuxnet specifically targeted Siemens PLCs (Programmable Logic Controllers) used in uranium enrichment centrifuges. It spread through infected USB drives and exploited multiple zero-day vulnerabilities in Windows to gain control over targeted systems. Once inside, Stuxnet manipulated centrifuge speeds, causing mechanical failures while reporting normal operations to monitoring systems. The attack is believed to be a joint effort by the U.S. and Israeli intelligence agencies. Stuxnet marked the beginning of cyber warfare targeting critical infrastructure and highlighted the vulnerabilities of industrial control systems to cyberattacks.

The Mirai botnet demonstrated the power of large-scale distributed denial-of-service (DDoS) attacks. In 2016, Mirai infected thousands of Internet of Things (IoT) devices, such as routers, IP cameras, and DVRs, turning them into bots used to launch massive DDoS attacks. By exploiting weak default passwords on IoT devices, Mirai built a botnet capable of overwhelming even the most resilient online services. One of its most notable attacks targeted Dyn, a major DNS provider, disrupting access to major websites such as Twitter, Netflix, and Reddit. The Mirai botnet's source code was later released publicly, leading to the creation of multiple variants used by cybercriminals worldwide. This attack exposed the security risks associated with IoT devices and the dangers of poor default configurations.

The SolarWinds supply chain attack, discovered in December 2020, revealed the risks of advanced nation-state cyber operations. Attackers compromised SolarWinds, a widely used IT management company, by injecting malicious code into its Orion software updates. When organizations installed these updates, they unknowingly introduced a backdoor, later known as Sunburst, into their networks. The attack affected thousands of organizations, including U.S. government agencies, Fortune 500 companies, and cybersecurity firms. Once inside, the attackers conducted stealthy reconnaissance, exfiltrating sensitive data over several months before the breach was discovered. The SolarWinds attack demonstrated the dangers of supply chain compromises and the need for stricter software integrity verification.

The Emotet malware campaign was one of the most persistent and dangerous banking trojans and botnets in history. Initially developed as a banking trojan in 2014, Emotet evolved into a modular malware platform used to deliver ransomware and other payloads. It spread primarily through malicious email attachments and embedded links, often using stolen email threads to appear more convincing. Once inside a network, Emotet used lateral movement techniques to infect additional machines and establish long-term persistence. In January

2021, an international law enforcement operation dismantled Emotet's infrastructure, disrupting one of the most prolific cybercrime operations. The Emotet case highlighted the importance of global collaboration in combating cyber threats and the need for advanced email security measures.

The Operation Aurora cyberattack, discovered in 2010, was a sophisticated campaign attributed to Chinese state-sponsored hackers. The attack targeted major technology companies, including Google, Adobe, and Intel, using advanced persistent threats (APTs) to steal intellectual property and sensitive data. Attackers exploited zero-day vulnerabilities in Internet Explorer to gain access to corporate networks, using spear phishing and social engineering techniques to infiltrate organizations. The attack led to significant geopolitical tensions, with Google publicly announcing its withdrawal from China due to cybersecurity concerns. Operation Aurora demonstrated the long-term risks posed by APT groups and the importance of securing critical intellectual property against cyber espionage.

The DarkSide ransomware attack on Colonial Pipeline in May 2021 disrupted fuel supply chains across the United States. The ransomware attack targeted Colonial Pipeline's IT infrastructure, forcing the company to shut down operations to prevent further damage. DarkSide, a ransomware-as-a-service (RaaS) group, encrypted critical files and demanded millions of dollars in Bitcoin ransom. The attack caused widespread panic, leading to fuel shortages and price spikes. Colonial Pipeline ultimately paid the ransom, but U.S. law enforcement later recovered part of the payment. This incident underscored the vulnerability of critical infrastructure to ransomware attacks and the debate over whether organizations should pay cybercriminals to restore operations.

The Kaseya VSA supply chain ransomware attack, carried out by the REvil ransomware group in July 2021, further demonstrated the dangers of supply chain vulnerabilities. Attackers exploited a zero-day vulnerability in Kaseya's VSA remote management software, delivering ransomware to managed service providers (MSPs) and their clients. The attack affected thousands of businesses, encrypting files and demanding ransom payments. Unlike previous ransomware attacks, REvil's strategy focused on mass exploitation through a single vulnerability, amplifying the scale of the attack. The incident highlighted the risks associated with remote management tools and the importance of patch management in preventing supply chain attacks.

Major malware attacks continue to evolve, leveraging sophisticated techniques to bypass security defenses. Each case study provides valuable lessons in threat detection, incident response, and cybersecurity resilience. By analyzing these incidents, organizations can adapt their security strategies, implement better defenses, and reduce the impact of future cyber threats. The continuous improvement of cybersecurity policies, technologies, and awareness is essential to staying ahead of cybercriminals and mitigating large-scale malware attacks.

Emerging Trends in Malware Development

Malware development continues to evolve as cybercriminals adapt to new security measures, technological advancements, and changes in user behavior. Attackers are constantly refining their techniques to evade detection, exploit vulnerabilities, and maximize their financial or strategic gains. Modern malware is more sophisticated, resilient, and difficult to analyze than ever before. Understanding emerging trends in malware development is essential for security professionals to anticipate new threats and enhance defensive strategies.

One of the most significant trends in modern malware development is the rise of fileless malware. Unlike traditional malware, which relies on executable files stored on disk, fileless malware operates entirely in memory. It often exploits legitimate system tools such as PowerShell, Windows Management Instrumentation (WMI), and Microsoft Office macros to execute malicious commands. Because fileless malware does not leave behind traditional file-based signatures, it is harder to detect using conventional antivirus solutions. Attackers increasingly favor fileless techniques to bypass security measures and maintain persistence on compromised systems.

The use of living-off-the-land binaries (LOLBins) has become another prevalent trend in malware development. Cybercriminals leverage legitimate system tools already present on a victim's machine to execute malicious payloads without downloading additional software. Attackers use tools such as certutil, mshta, rundll32, and wmic to perform malicious actions, making it more challenging for security solutions to differentiate between legitimate and malicious activity. Since these tools are signed by Microsoft and commonly used for administrative tasks, they often bypass traditional security controls.

Malware developers are increasingly incorporating artificial intelligence (AI) and machine learning (ML) evasion techniques into their attacks. Some malware variants use AI-powered decision-making to determine the best method for infecting a target, adapting their behavior based on security controls detected on the system. Additionally, adversarial machine learning techniques allow malware to bypass security models by identifying and exploiting weaknesses in AI-driven detection algorithms. As AI becomes more integrated into cybersecurity defenses, cybercriminals are actively developing methods to counteract these advanced protections.

Ransomware evolution remains a significant concern in malware development. Traditional ransomware attacks focused on encrypting files and demanding payment for decryption. However, modern ransomware operators have adopted double extortion and triple extortion tactics. In double extortion, attackers not only encrypt files but also exfiltrate sensitive data, threatening to release it publicly if the ransom is not paid. Triple extortion goes a step further by adding pressure through additional means, such as Distributed Denial of Service (DDoS) attacks or direct threats to business partners. Ransomware-as-a-service (RaaS) models have also emerged, enabling cybercriminals with little technical expertise to launch sophisticated attacks using prebuilt ransomware kits provided by experienced developers.

The increasing use of advanced obfuscation and encryption techniques has made malware harder to detect and analyze. Attackers employ polymorphic and metamorphic malware that continuously changes its code to evade signature-based detection. Polymorphic malware modifies itself slightly with each execution, while metamorphic malware completely rewrites its code while maintaining the same functionality. Additionally, malware developers use techniques such as packing, runtime encryption, and code injection to hide malicious payloads from static and dynamic analysis tools.

Cloud-based malware is becoming more prevalent as organizations migrate their infrastructure to cloud environments. Attackers target cloud services, misconfigured storage buckets, and virtualized environments to deploy malware that can propagate across multiple instances. Cloud-based malware often leverages legitimate cloud services such as Google Drive, Dropbox, and AWS to host malicious payloads, making detection more difficult. Additionally, attackers exploit weak identity and access management (IAM) policies to gain persistence in cloud environments.

Mobile malware continues to grow as cybercriminals focus on Android and iOS devices. With the widespread use of mobile applications for banking, communication, and business operations, attackers see smartphones as valuable targets. Mobile malware often masquerades as legitimate applications on third-party app stores, luring victims into downloading infected software. Banking trojans, spyware, and SMS-based phishing (smishing) campaigns are frequently used to steal credentials, intercept messages, and monitor user activity. Attackers also exploit zero-day vulnerabilities in mobile operating systems to gain remote access and control over infected devices.

Supply chain attacks have become a preferred method for malware distribution. Instead of targeting individual users or organizations, attackers compromise software vendors or service providers to distribute malware through legitimate updates. High-profile supply chain attacks, such as the SolarWinds and Kaseya incidents, have demonstrated how a single compromised update can infect thousands of organizations. Malware developers continue to refine their tactics, targeting widely used software platforms and hardware components to maximize their reach.

The integration of blockchain and cryptocurrency in malware operations has changed the way cybercriminals conduct financial transactions. Ransomware payments, illicit trading, and underground markets have shifted to cryptocurrency to maintain anonymity. Additionally, attackers are deploying cryptojacking malware, which secretly uses victims' computing resources to mine cryptocurrencies. Cryptojacking is difficult to detect because it does not cause immediate damage but instead degrades system performance over time. Malware developers are also leveraging blockchain technology to create decentralized command-and-control (C2) infrastructures, making takedowns more challenging for law enforcement.

The rise of nation-state malware and cyber warfare highlights the increasing role of state-sponsored cyberattacks in geopolitical conflicts. Nation-state actors develop advanced persistent threats (APTs) with sophisticated capabilities for espionage, sabotage, and disruption. These malware campaigns often target critical infrastructure, government agencies, and military organizations. Cyber warfare tactics include data theft, industrial sabotage, and the deployment of destructive malware such as Stuxnet, NotPetya, and Industroyer. As geopolitical tensions rise, the development of offensive cyber capabilities continues to escalate.

Malware targeting AI-powered voice assistants and IoT devices is another emerging trend. With the proliferation of smart home devices, attackers are developing malware that exploits voice-controlled systems such as Amazon Alexa, Google Assistant, and Apple Siri. IoT malware infects connected devices such as security cameras, smart TVs, and industrial sensors, turning them into botnets for large-scale DDoS attacks. As more devices become interconnected, the attack surface for malware developers expands, making IoT security a growing concern.

Malware developers are also focusing on cross-platform infections, creating malware that can execute on multiple operating systems. Traditionally, malware was designed for specific platforms such as Windows or Linux. However, modern threats leverage cross-platform frameworks such as Golang and Python to create adaptable malware that can infect Windows, macOS, and Linux systems simultaneously.

Attackers use these techniques to maximize the reach of their campaigns and increase the difficulty of detection and remediation.

The automation of malware attacks using AI and botnets is making cybercrime more efficient and scalable. Attackers are leveraging AI-driven bots to conduct automated phishing campaigns, exploit vulnerabilities in real time, and evade security defenses. AI-powered malware adapts to changing environments, making detection and response more challenging. Automated exploitation frameworks allow cybercriminals to scan for vulnerabilities, deploy malware payloads, and control infected devices with minimal human intervention.

As malware development continues to advance, cybersecurity professionals must stay ahead by adopting proactive defense strategies, leveraging AI-driven security tools, and improving threat intelligence sharing. The evolving landscape of cyber threats requires continuous research, adaptation, and collaboration among security experts to mitigate the risks posed by emerging malware trends.

Malware Analysis in Threat Hunting

Threat hunting is a proactive cybersecurity approach that involves actively searching for hidden threats within an organization's network. Unlike traditional reactive security measures that rely on alerts and automated detection, threat hunting focuses on identifying unknown or advanced threats that may have bypassed existing defenses. Malware analysis plays a crucial role in this process, providing the intelligence needed to detect, analyze, and mitigate sophisticated malware threats before they cause significant damage. By integrating malware analysis into threat hunting, security teams gain deeper insights into attacker tactics, techniques, and procedures (TTPs), allowing them to uncover hidden infections and improve overall cybersecurity resilience.

Malware analysis in threat hunting begins with the collection of suspicious artifacts, such as files, processes, network traffic, and log data. Threat hunters leverage various data sources, including endpoint detection and response (EDR) solutions, intrusion detection systems

(IDS), security information and event management (SIEM) platforms, and threat intelligence feeds. Suspicious indicators, such as abnormal network connections, unusual system modifications, or unexpected process executions, serve as starting points for deeper investigation. Once a potential threat is identified, malware analysis techniques are used to determine the nature of the malicious activity and assess its impact.

Static analysis is one of the first steps in analyzing malware during threat hunting. Without executing the malware, analysts examine file attributes, metadata, embedded strings, and cryptographic hashes to identify known malware variants. Tools such as PEStudio, YARA, and VirusTotal help analyze binary files and detect signatures that match previously identified threats. Static analysis also reveals potential IoCs, such as hardcoded IP addresses, suspicious API calls, and registry modifications. By applying YARA rules to large datasets, threat hunters can quickly detect and classify malware samples that exhibit similar characteristics.

Dynamic analysis provides deeper insights into how malware behaves when executed in a controlled environment. Sandboxing solutions such as Cuckoo Sandbox allow analysts to run malware samples in isolated virtual machines and observe their runtime behavior. Threat hunters use sandbox reports to identify file modifications, process injections, network communications, and persistence mechanisms. Analyzing behavioral indicators helps determine whether a suspicious file is actively attempting to evade detection, escalate privileges, or communicate with a command-and-control (C2) server. By correlating sandbox results with network logs, analysts can track malware propagation and containment strategies.

Memory forensics plays a vital role in malware analysis within threat hunting. Many advanced threats operate entirely in memory to avoid detection by traditional antivirus solutions. Threat hunters use tools such as Volatility to extract forensic artifacts from memory dumps, revealing hidden processes, injected code, and decrypted payloads. Memory analysis is particularly effective against fileless malware, which does not leave traditional file-based signatures but instead executes malicious code directly within legitimate system processes. By examining memory structures and process relationships, threat hunters can uncover stealthy infections that evade conventional security controls.

Network traffic analysis is another essential component of malware analysis in threat hunting. Malware often relies on network communication to exfiltrate data, receive commands, or download additional payloads. Threat hunters monitor DNS requests, HTTP headers, encrypted SSL/TLS traffic, and anomalous data flows to identify suspicious activity. Tools such as Wireshark, Zeek (formerly Bro), and Suricata help detect malware-related network patterns, such as beaconing behavior, domain generation algorithms (DGA), and unauthorized external connections. By analyzing network traffic, security teams can trace malware infections back to their initial entry points and implement countermeasures to disrupt ongoing attacks.

Reverse engineering techniques enhance threat hunting by providing a deeper understanding of how malware operates. By disassembling and debugging malicious code, analysts can uncover its true functionality, identify exploited vulnerabilities, and extract encryption keys or decryption routines. Tools such as IDA Pro, Ghidra, OllyDbg, and x64dbg help analysts analyze compiled binaries, reconstruct attack chains, and develop signatures for future detections. Reverse engineering is particularly valuable for analyzing advanced persistent threats (APTs) and zero-day exploits, where attackers use custom malware to evade traditional detection methods.

Threat intelligence integration enhances the effectiveness of malware analysis in threat hunting. By correlating findings with known threat actor campaigns, security teams can attribute attacks, predict future attack vectors, and implement proactive defenses. Platforms such as MITRE ATT&CK, MISP, and Open Threat Exchange (OTX) provide threat intelligence feeds that help analysts track adversary tactics and IoCs. By continuously updating detection rules and security policies based on intelligence-driven analysis, organizations can stay ahead of emerging threats and reduce their exposure to malware attacks.

Automating malware analysis in threat hunting improves efficiency and scalability. Security teams use scripts and custom tools written in Python, PowerShell, and Bash to automate malware triage, log analysis, and forensic data extraction. Machine learning models enhance malware detection by identifying patterns in large datasets and flagging anomalies that indicate malicious behavior. Automated threat hunting frameworks leverage AI-driven analytics to detect malware variants that exhibit subtle deviations from normal system activity. By reducing manual effort, automation allows threat hunters to focus on high-priority investigations and complex threat scenarios.

Threat hunting also involves identifying and mitigating persistence mechanisms used by malware to maintain long-term access to compromised systems. Malware often modifies registry keys, creates scheduled tasks, or implants backdoors to survive system reboots and security scans. Threat hunters analyze system logs, startup configurations, and Active Directory events to detect unauthorized modifications. By removing persistence mechanisms and implementing endpoint hardening measures, security teams prevent attackers from re-establishing control over infected systems.

Incident response and remediation strategies are closely linked to malware analysis in threat hunting. Once a malicious artifact is confirmed, security teams must contain the threat, remove infected files, and restore affected systems. Threat hunters provide forensic evidence to incident responders, enabling them to trace the full scope of an attack, identify compromised accounts, and implement corrective actions. By documenting findings and updating security controls, organizations improve their overall resilience against future malware infections.

Collaboration between threat hunters, malware analysts, and security operations center (SOC) teams strengthens an organization's security posture. Effective threat hunting relies on knowledge-sharing, real-time intelligence updates, and cross-functional expertise. Security teams participate in tabletop exercises, red teaming simulations, and blue team defensive strategies to refine their malware detection and response capabilities. By fostering a proactive security culture, organizations can detect malware infections early, minimize dwell time, and disrupt attack campaigns before they escalate.

Malware analysis in threat hunting is a continuous process that evolves with emerging cyber threats. Attackers constantly develop new evasion techniques, making it essential for threat hunters to adapt their methodologies and tools. By leveraging advanced malware analysis techniques, integrating threat intelligence, and automating repetitive tasks, security teams enhance their ability to detect and neutralize sophisticated threats. Proactive threat hunting not only improves malware detection rates but also strengthens an organization's overall cybersecurity resilience, ensuring a more robust defense against modern cyber threats.

Red Team vs Blue Team Perspectives on Malware

Malware is a critical component of cybersecurity operations, affecting both offensive and defensive strategies. Within cybersecurity, Red Teams and Blue Teams approach malware from different perspectives. The Red Team, acting as ethical hackers, simulates real-world cyberattacks using malware to test an organization's defenses. The Blue Team, responsible for cybersecurity defense, focuses on detecting, analyzing, and mitigating malware threats. Understanding these two perspectives provides valuable insights into how malware is used for both offensive security testing and defensive threat response.

The Red Team's primary goal is to emulate adversaries by testing an organization's security posture. Red Team members design and deploy custom malware to infiltrate networks, bypass security controls, and maintain persistence within the environment. They create payloads that mimic real-world threats, such as trojans, ransomware, and backdoors, to evaluate an organization's ability to detect and respond to an attack. By using techniques similar to those employed by cybercriminals, the Red Team identifies vulnerabilities and weaknesses that could be exploited in a real attack scenario.

Red Team operators often develop and use custom malware that avoids detection by traditional security tools. They employ techniques such as fileless execution, code injection, and living-off-the-land binaries (LOLBins) to evade endpoint protection solutions. Red Team malware typically leverages obfuscation and encryption to avoid triggering antivirus and endpoint detection and response (EDR) systems. Advanced payloads include modular malware that adapts to different environments and establishes persistence without raising alarms. By using these techniques, Red Teams assess how well an organization can detect, analyze, and mitigate sophisticated threats.

One of the most common Red Team malware deployment methods is phishing. Red Team operators craft convincing phishing emails that contain malicious attachments or links leading to weaponized payloads. These payloads execute remote access trojans (RATs), keyloggers, or other forms of malware that allow the Red Team to maintain access to a compromised system. Social engineering tactics play a significant role in Red Team operations, as real-world attackers frequently use similar methods to infiltrate networks.

The Red Team also tests post-exploitation techniques once malware is successfully deployed. This includes privilege escalation, lateral movement, and data exfiltration. By moving through the network undetected, the Red Team evaluates how well the Blue Team can detect and respond to malicious activity. They use tools like Cobalt Strike, Metasploit, and Empire to simulate advanced persistent threats (APTs), testing whether security monitoring solutions can detect these threats in real time. If the Blue Team fails to detect Red Team activity, it highlights weaknesses in threat detection capabilities.

From the Blue Team's perspective, malware represents a persistent and evolving threat that requires continuous monitoring and analysis. The Blue Team is responsible for defending against real-world malware attacks by implementing security controls, detecting anomalies, and responding to incidents. They use a combination of static and dynamic malware analysis, threat intelligence, and behavioral analytics to identify and mitigate malware infections.

Blue Team analysts rely on endpoint detection and response (EDR) solutions, security information and event management (SIEM) systems, and intrusion detection systems (IDS) to monitor for signs of malware activity. They look for unusual process executions, suspicious network connections, and unauthorized system modifications. By analyzing indicators of compromise (IoCs), such as file hashes, registry changes, and C2 communications, the Blue Team can identify and contain malware infections before they spread.

A key challenge for the Blue Team is distinguishing between Red Team activity and actual cyber threats. During Red Team engagements, the Blue Team must analyze attack patterns to determine whether an intrusion is a simulated test or a real attack. Effective communication between Red and Blue Teams ensures that defensive strategies improve without disrupting business operations. The Blue Team uses the data collected during Red Team exercises to enhance detection rules, refine incident response procedures, and improve threat-hunting capabilities.

The Blue Team employs malware reverse engineering to understand how malicious code operates and how to develop countermeasures. Using tools such as IDA Pro, Ghidra, and x64dbg, they analyze Red Team malware to uncover obfuscation techniques, execution flows, and persistence mechanisms. Reverse engineering provides insights into how attackers modify their techniques over time, helping Blue Teams stay ahead of emerging threats.

Behavioral analysis plays a critical role in malware detection. Instead of relying solely on signatures, the Blue Team focuses on identifying malicious behaviors, such as unauthorized process creation, unusual system file modifications, and abnormal user activity. By using machine learning and AI-driven detection models, the Blue Team can detect previously unknown malware variants based on behavioral patterns. Advanced threat-hunting techniques allow the Blue Team to proactively search for malware before it triggers security alerts.

Incident response is a core function of the Blue Team when malware infections occur. Once malware is detected, the Blue Team isolates affected systems, conducts forensic analysis, and removes malicious components. They use memory forensics tools like Volatility to extract malware artifacts from infected machines, helping to reconstruct the attack timeline. The Blue Team also updates security policies, firewall rules, and intrusion prevention systems (IPS) based on the findings from malware incidents.

Threat intelligence sharing is another important aspect of the Blue Team's malware defense strategy. By collaborating with external organizations, security researchers, and industry groups, the Blue Team stays informed about new malware threats and attack techniques. Platforms such as MITRE ATT&CK, MISP, and VirusTotal provide valuable intelligence on emerging threats, allowing the Blue Team to refine their detection and response strategies. Sharing IoCs and threat reports ensures that other organizations can also defend against similar attacks.

Purple Teaming is an approach that combines both Red and Blue Team perspectives to improve cybersecurity effectiveness. Instead of working separately, the Red and Blue Teams collaborate to enhance detection and response capabilities. The Red Team shares attack techniques with the Blue Team, allowing defenders to develop real-time countermeasures. This iterative process helps organizations build stronger security defenses, ensuring that detection capabilities evolve alongside adversarial tactics.

Malware analysis from both Red Team and Blue Team perspectives is essential for strengthening cybersecurity defenses. The Red Team's role in simulating real-world attacks helps organizations identify weaknesses and improve security measures. Meanwhile, the Blue Team's focus on detection, analysis, and response ensures that organizations are prepared to handle actual malware threats. By leveraging the insights gained from both offensive and defensive perspectives, organizations can develop more effective strategies to detect, analyze, and mitigate malware threats in an ever-evolving cyber landscape.

Building a Malware Analysis Lab

A well-structured malware analysis lab is essential for safely studying and dissecting malicious software without risking unintentional infections or data leaks. A properly configured lab provides analysts with a controlled environment where they can analyze malware samples, observe behaviors, and develop defensive strategies. Whether for static analysis, dynamic execution, or reverse engineering, a malware lab must be designed with security, isolation, and flexibility in mind to handle different types of threats effectively.

The foundation of a malware analysis lab begins with hardware and virtualization. Instead of using physical machines, analysts rely on virtual machines (VMs) to create isolated environments for executing and analyzing malware safely. Virtualization platforms such as VMware Workstation, VirtualBox, and KVM allow for quick deployment and restoration of infected environments. Analysts can take snapshots of clean system states before running malware, ensuring that they can revert to a safe state after analysis. Multiple VMs with different operating systems, including Windows, Linux, and macOS, provide a diverse environment for testing various malware strains.

Network isolation is a critical security measure in a malware lab. Malware often communicates with external servers for command-and-control (C2) instructions, data exfiltration, or further payload downloads. Allowing uncontrolled network access can lead to unintentional infections spreading beyond the lab. Analysts configure internal networks using tools such as INetSim, which simulates internet services locally, preventing malware from reaching real C2 servers. Additionally, network monitoring solutions such as Wireshark and Zeek capture and analyze traffic, providing insights into malware communication patterns. A firewall or proxy server is used to restrict internet access while logging outgoing requests for further investigation.

A Windows-based malware analysis environment is necessary, as most malware targets the Windows operating system. A dedicated VM running a vulnerable or older version of Windows allows analysts to study exploits and privilege escalation techniques. Analysts install debugging and monitoring tools such as Process Monitor, Process Explorer, Autoruns, and Regshot to track system modifications. Sysmon is also configured to provide detailed logging of system activity, including file changes, process injections, and network connections. These tools help identify the impact of malware on a system and determine persistence mechanisms.

For dynamic analysis, sandboxes such as Cuckoo Sandbox allow for automated malware execution in a controlled environment. Cuckoo captures file modifications, API calls, network traffic, and process interactions, generating detailed reports on malware behavior. Running malware in a sandbox helps analysts determine whether it exhibits persistence, evasion techniques, or signs of ransomware activity. By integrating YARA rules, analysts can classify malware into known families based on behavioral patterns and extracted strings.

Static analysis tools are essential for examining malware samples without executing them. PEStudio allows analysts to inspect Portable Executable (PE) file headers, imported functions, and embedded resources. Strings extraction tools such as FLOSS and BinText reveal hardcoded IP addresses, URLs, or encryption keys. The use of pefile in Python enables automated parsing of malware binaries, providing insights into their structure and functionality. Static analysis serves as the first layer of investigation, allowing analysts to determine whether further dynamic execution is necessary.

For reverse engineering, the lab must include tools for disassembling and debugging malware binaries. IDA Pro and Ghidra provide in-depth static code analysis, enabling analysts to decompile and study malware logic. Debuggers such as x64dbg and OllyDbg allow for real-time execution tracking, helping analysts identify obfuscation techniques and unpack encrypted payloads. Reverse engineering helps extract encryption keys, identify vulnerabilities, and understand how malware interacts with system components.

The lab also requires memory forensics capabilities to analyze malware that operates in RAM. Volatility Framework is an essential tool for extracting process lists, injected code, and registry modifications from memory dumps. Fileless malware and advanced persistent threats (APTs) often execute solely in memory, making traditional disk forensics ineffective. Memory analysis allows analysts to recover artifacts that may not exist in traditional logs or disk-based investigations.

To safely store and manage malware samples, analysts use dedicated repositories such as Viper or Malware Bazaar. Samples are stored in encrypted archives with strong passwords to prevent accidental execution. Analysts use virtual machines with restricted permissions to handle and categorize malware files. Hashing techniques ensure that samples are not modified or tampered with, preserving their integrity for future research. A structured malware database helps track relationships between samples, identify similarities, and correlate findings with threat intelligence sources.

The lab must also include threat intelligence integration to enrich analysis with external data sources. Platforms such as VirusTotal, MISP, and AlienVault OTX provide reputation checks for file hashes, IP addresses, and domains associated with malware. Analysts use APIs to automate lookups, cross-referencing malware samples with known threat reports. Intelligence sharing enables organizations to contribute and receive real-time updates on emerging threats, improving overall security awareness.

To simulate real-world attack scenarios, Red Team tools such as Cobalt Strike and Metasploit are used to test malware execution and evasion techniques. By deploying simulated attacks in a controlled environment, analysts assess how different security solutions respond to various threat vectors. This approach allows defenders to refine detection signatures, improve endpoint protection, and enhance threat-hunting strategies.

A well-documented incident response plan is necessary for handling potential lab breaches or misconfigurations. Analysts must follow strict protocols for isolating infected systems, preventing accidental malware execution outside the lab, and responding to potential security incidents. Regular training and drills ensure that team members are prepared to handle malware safely and efficiently.

Security in the malware lab extends to operational security (OPSEC) measures. Analysts use dedicated workstations or air-gapped systems to prevent accidental data leaks. Lab systems do not connect to production networks, and malware samples are handled with strict access controls. Analysts use VPNs and anonymization tools when interacting with threat intelligence platforms to avoid revealing their real identities to potential adversaries.

Building an effective malware analysis lab requires careful planning, robust security measures, and the right combination of tools and techniques. A well-equipped lab enables analysts to safely study malware, understand its behavior, and develop countermeasures to protect against evolving threats. By continuously refining the lab environment and adopting new technologies, security professionals enhance their ability to analyze, detect, and respond to malware attacks.

Future of Malware and Cybersecurity Defense

The future of malware and cybersecurity defense is constantly evolving as technology advances and cybercriminal tactics become more sophisticated. Attackers continuously develop new ways to bypass security measures, exploit vulnerabilities, and achieve their malicious objectives. In response, cybersecurity professionals must anticipate emerging threats and adapt their defense strategies to stay ahead of adversaries. The intersection of artificial intelligence, automation, and evolving attack techniques will shape the future landscape of cybersecurity, requiring organizations to enhance their security posture through proactive threat detection, response, and mitigation.

One of the most significant trends in the future of malware is the increasing use of artificial intelligence and machine learning to enhance attack capabilities. Cybercriminals are leveraging AI to create malware that can dynamically adapt to security defenses, making detection more difficult. AI-powered malware can analyze its environment, modify its behavior, and evade traditional security solutions by learning from how security tools respond. For example, malware may use machine learning models to determine the best infection method, adjust encryption techniques, and detect whether it is running in a sandbox environment. As AI technology continues to improve, attackers will develop more autonomous and resilient malware strains.

The rise of highly targeted and sophisticated attacks, often referred to as advanced persistent threats (APTs), will continue to be a major challenge for cybersecurity defenses. State-sponsored cyber operations, cyber espionage campaigns, and financially motivated threat actors will increasingly focus on long-term infiltration of high-value targets. APT groups use custom-built malware, zero-day exploits, and stealthy persistence techniques to maintain access to compromised systems for extended periods. Organizations must enhance their threat intelligence capabilities and adopt proactive threat-hunting approaches to detect APT activity before it causes severe damage.

Another key trend in malware development is the growing focus on fileless and memory-resident malware. Traditional malware typically relies on executable files stored on disk, which can be detected through antivirus scans and static analysis. However, fileless malware operates entirely in system memory, leveraging legitimate system tools such as PowerShell, Windows Management Instrumentation (WMI), and macros to execute malicious code. This approach allows malware to bypass signature-based detection methods and persist without leaving traces on disk. Security solutions must evolve to incorporate behavioral analysis and memory forensics to detect and respond to fileless threats effectively.

Ransomware attacks will continue to evolve, with cybercriminals adopting more aggressive extortion techniques. The traditional ransomware model of encrypting files and demanding payment has expanded into double and triple extortion. Double extortion involves exfiltrating sensitive data before encryption, threatening to release it publicly if the ransom is not paid. Triple extortion adds further pressure by launching distributed denial-of-service (DDoS) attacks or directly targeting customers and stakeholders of the victim organization. The future of ransomware defense will require a combination of strong backup solutions, real-time threat intelligence, and international law enforcement collaboration to disrupt ransomware groups.

The increasing adoption of cloud computing and hybrid work environments presents new challenges for cybersecurity defenses. As organizations migrate workloads to cloud infrastructure, attackers are shifting their focus to cloud-based malware and misconfigured cloud services. Cloud malware can exploit weak identity and access management (IAM) policies, insecure APIs, and poorly configured storage solutions to gain unauthorized access. Defending against cloud-based threats requires organizations to implement robust identity protection measures, enforce least-privilege access, and continuously monitor cloud environments for suspicious activity.

Supply chain attacks are expected to become more frequent and impactful in the future. Instead of directly targeting high-security organizations, attackers compromise software vendors, hardware manufacturers, or third-party service providers to distribute malware. The SolarWinds and Kaseya attacks demonstrated the devastating consequences of supply chain compromises, affecting thousands of organizations worldwide. Strengthening supply chain security will require enhanced software integrity verification, stricter vendor security assessments, and real-time monitoring of third-party dependencies.

Cybercriminals are increasingly using blockchain and cryptocurrency technologies to facilitate illegal activities while maintaining anonymity. Ransomware payments, illicit marketplaces, and malware monetization strategies rely on decentralized financial systems to evade detection. Additionally, attackers are exploring blockchain-based command-and-control (C2) mechanisms, making it more difficult for security researchers and law enforcement to track and disrupt malicious operations. Defending against these threats will require improved cryptocurrency transaction tracking, stronger regulatory frameworks, and enhanced blockchain security measures.

The expansion of the Internet of Things (IoT) and connected devices introduces new attack vectors for malware. Many IoT devices lack robust security features, making them easy targets for botnets and large-scale cyberattacks. IoT malware, such as the Mirai botnet, exploits weak default credentials and unpatched vulnerabilities to compromise devices, which can then be used for DDoS attacks or unauthorized surveillance. Future cybersecurity strategies must include improved IoT security standards, automatic patching mechanisms, and AI-driven anomaly detection to mitigate IoT-based threats.

The convergence of malware with deepfake and social engineering techniques represents a growing cybersecurity risk. Attackers are using AI-generated deepfake videos, voice cloning, and sophisticated phishing techniques to manipulate users into downloading malware or disclosing sensitive information. As these social engineering tactics become more convincing, organizations will need to invest in user awareness training, biometric authentication solutions, and AI-driven fraud detection to counteract these threats.

Defensive cybersecurity measures will increasingly rely on AI and automation to combat evolving malware threats. AI-powered security solutions can analyze vast amounts of data, identify anomalies, and detect malicious activity in real time. Automated security orchestration, automation, and response (SOAR) platforms enable faster incident response by automating threat detection, investigation, and remediation workflows. The future of cybersecurity defense will require a balance between human expertise and AI-driven automation to stay ahead of rapidly evolving cyber threats.

As quantum computing technology advances, it poses both opportunities and challenges for malware and cybersecurity. Quantum computers have the potential to break traditional encryption algorithms, rendering current cryptographic defenses obsolete. Cybercriminals may leverage quantum computing to develop new forms of malware capable of bypassing modern security controls. To prepare for this emerging threat, organizations must invest in quantum-resistant cryptography, explore post-quantum security frameworks, and collaborate with research institutions to develop next-generation encryption standards.

International collaboration and cybersecurity regulations will play a crucial role in shaping the future of malware defense. Governments, private sector organizations, and cybersecurity researchers must work together to establish global cybersecurity frameworks, enforce stricter data protection laws, and coordinate threat intelligence sharing. Increased investment in public-private partnerships and cybersecurity education programs will help build a more resilient digital ecosystem capable of defending against advanced malware threats.

The future of malware and cybersecurity defense will be defined by the continuous battle between attackers and defenders. As cyber threats become more sophisticated, organizations must adopt a proactive approach that combines AI-driven threat detection, strong encryption, cloud security, and advanced behavioral analysis. The cybersecurity landscape will continue to evolve, requiring ongoing innovation, collaboration, and investment in cutting-edge security technologies to mitigate emerging malware threats effectively.